This is part of a true story of an Indian girl abandoned on an island. She lived there alone for eighteen years. In this part of the story she decides to attack the wild dogs which threaten her. The leader of the pack, a big dog with yellow eyes, is her main target.

The story is taken from a book called *Island of the Blue Dolphins* by Scott O'Dell.

There had been wild dogs on the Island of the Blue Dolphins as long as I remember, but after the Aleuts had slain most of the men of our tribe and their dogs had left to join the others, the pack became much bolder. It spent the nights running through the village and during the day was never far off. It was then that we made plans to get rid of them, but the ship came and everyone left Ghalas-at.

I am sure that the pack grew bolder because of their leader, the big one with the thick fur around his neck and the yellow eyes.

I had never seen this dog before the Aleuts came and no one else had, so he must have come with them and been left behind when they sailed away. He was a much larger dog than any of ours, which besides have short hair and brown eyes. I was sure that he was an Aleut dog.

Already I had killed five of the pack, but there were many left, more than in the beginning, for some had been born in the meantime. The young dogs were even wilder than the old ones.

I first went to the hill near the cave when the pack was away and collected armloads of brush which I placed near the mouth of their lair. Then I waited until the pack was in the cave. It went there early in the morning to sleep after it had spent the night prowling. I took with me the big bow and five arrows and two of the spears. I went quietly, circling around the mouth of the cave and came up to it from the side. There I left all of my weapons except one spear.

I set fire to the brush and pushed it into the cave. If the wild dogs heard me, there was no sound from them. Near by was a ledge of rock which I climbed, taking my weapons with me.

The fire burned high. Some of the smoke trailed out over the hill, but much of it stayed in the cave. Soon the pack would have to leave. I did not hope to kill more than five of them because I had only that many arrows, but if the leader was one of the five I would be satisfied. It might be wiser if I waited and saved all my arrows for him, and this I decided to do.

None of the dogs appeared before the fire died. Then three ran out and away. Seven more followed and a long time afterwards a like number. There were many more still left in the cave.

The leader came next. Unlike the others, he did not run away. He jumped over the ashes and stood at the mouth of the cave, sniffing the air. I was so close to him that I could see his nose quivering, but he did not see me until I raised my bow. Fortunately I did not frighten him.

He stood facing me, his front legs spread as if he were ready to spring, his yellow eyes narrowed to slits. The arrow struck him in the chest. He turned away from me, took one step and fell. I sent another arrow towards him which went wide.

At this time three more dogs trotted out of the cave. I used the last of my arrows and killed two of them.

Carrying both of the spears, I climbed down from the ledge and went through the brush to the place where the leader had fallen. He was not there. While I had been shooting at the other dogs, he had gone. He could not have gone far because of his wound, but though I looked everywhere, around the ledge where I had been standing and in front of the cave, I did not find him.

I waited for a long time and then went inside the cave. It was deep, but I could see clearly.

Far back in a corner was the half-eaten carcass of a fox. Beside it was a black dog with four grey pups. One of the pups came slowly towards me, a round ball of fur that I could have held in my hand. I wanted to hold it, but the mother leaped to her feet and bared her teeth. I raised my spear as I backed out of the cave, yet I did not use it. The wounded leader was not there.

Night was coming and I left the cave, going along the foot of the hill that led to the cliff. I had not gone far on this trail that the wild dogs used when I saw the broken shaft of an arrow. I had been gnawed off near the tip and I knew it was from the arrow which had wounded the leader.

Farther on I saw his tracks in the dust. They were uneven as if he were travelling slowly. I followed them towards the cliff, but finally lost them in the darkness.

The next day and the next it rained and I did not go to look for him. I spent those days making more arrows, and on the third day, with these arrows and my spear, I went out along the trail the wild dogs had made to and from my house.

There were no tracks after the rain, but I followed the trail to the pile of rocks where I had seen them before. On the far side of the rocks I found the big grey dog. He had the broken arrow in his chest and he was lying with one of his legs under him.

He was about ten paces from me so I could see him clearly. I was sure that he was dead, but I lifted the spear and took good aim at him. Just as I was about to throw the spear, he raised his head a little from the earth and then let it drop.

This surprised me greatly and I stood there for a while not knowing what to do, whether to use the spear or my bow. I was used to animals playing dead until they suddenly turned on you or ran away.

The spear was the better of the two weapons at this distance, but I could not use it as well as the other, so I climbed on to the rocks where I could see him if he ran. I placed my feet carefully. I had a second arrow ready should I need it. I fitted an arrow and pulled back the string, aiming at his head.

Why I did not send the arrow I cannot say. I stood on the rock with the bow pulled back and my hand would not let it go. The big dog lay there and did not move and this may be the reason. If he had got up I would have killed him. I stood there for a long time looking down at him and then I climbed off the rocks.

He did not move when I went up to him, nor could I see him breathing until I was very close. The head of the arrow was in his chest and the broken shaft was covered with blood. The thick fur around his neck was matted from the rain.

I do not think that he knew I was picking him up, for his body was limp, as if he were dead. He was very heavy and the only way I could lift him was by kneeling and putting his legs around my shoulders.

In this manner, stopping to rest when I was tired, I carried him to the headland.

I could not get through the opening under the fence, so I cut the bindings and lifted out two of the whale ribs and thus took him into the house. He did not look at me or raise his head when I laid him on the floor, but his mouth was open and he was breathing.

The arrow had a small point, which was fortunate, and came out easily though it had gone deep. He did not move while I did this, nor afterwards as I cleaned the wound with a peeled stick from a coral bush. This bush has poisonous berries, yet its wood often heals wounds that nothing else will.

I had not gathered food for many days and the baskets were empty, so I left water for the dog and, after mending the fence, went down to the sea. I had no thought that he would live and I did not care.

All day I was among the rocks gathering shellfish and only once did I think of the wounded dog, my enemy, lying there in the house, and then to wonder why I had not killed him.

He was still alive when I got back, though he had not moved from the place where I had left him. Again I cleaned the wound with a coral twig. I then lifted his head and put water in his mouth, which he swallowed. This was the first time that he had looked at me since the time I had found him on the trail. His eyes were sunken and they looked out at me from far back in his head.

Before I went to sleep I gave him more water. In the morning I left food for him when I went down to the sea, and when I came home he had eaten it. He was lying in the corner, watching me. While I made a fire and cooked my supper, he watched me. His yellow eyes followed me wherever I moved.

That night I slept on the rock, for I was afraid of him, and at dawn as I went out I left the hole under the fence open so he could go. But he was there when I got back, lying in the sun with his head on his paws. I had speared two fish, which I cooked for my supper. Since he was very thin, I gave him one of them, and after he had eaten it he came over and lay down by the fire, watching me with his yellow eyes that were very narrow and slanted up at the corners.

Four nights I slept on the rock, and every morning I left the hole under the fence open so he could leave. Each day I speared a fish for him

and when I got home he was always at the fence waiting for it. He would not take the fish from me so I had to put it on the ground. Once I held my hand out to him, but at this he backed away and showed his teeth.

On the fourth day when I came back from the rocks early he was not there at the fence waiting. A strange feeling came over me. Always before when I returned, I had hoped that he would be gone. But now as I crawled under the fence I did not feel the same.

I called out, 'Dog, Dog,' for I had no other name for him.

I ran towards the house, calling it. He was inside. He was just getting to his feet, stretching himself and yawning. He looked first at the fish I carried and then at me and moved his tail.

That night I stayed in the house. Before I fell asleep I thought of a name for him, for I could not call him Dog. The name I thought of was Rontu, which means in our language Fox Eyes.

To think and talk about

A 1. How do you think the wild dogs had annoyed the girl?
   2. Why do you think she didn't send the arrow and kill the dog?
   3. 'I had no thought that he would live and I did not care.' Do you think she really means this? What do you think about what she says here?
   4. What showed that the dog was beginning to get better?
   5. Why did the girl decide to stop sleeping on the rock, and come into the house?
   6. The girl left the fence open to allow the dog to leave. Why do you think she is allowing her enemy his freedom?

B 1. What would you have done to the dog?
   2. 'Always before when I returned I had hoped that he would be gone. But now, as I crawled under the fence I did not feel the same.' How do you think she feels?
   3. What sort of life do you think the girl leads?
   4. The girl is alone on the island. How do you think this happened?
   5. Why didn't the dog leave when he was better?
   6. What do you think of the name she gave the dog? What name would you have given it?

More books to read

1. *The Black Pearl* by Scott O'Dell
   As a child Ramon knew the stories of the Manta Diablo — a mighty devilfish. Little did he know that he would struggle with this mighty fish to win from it the black pearl.

2. *The Pinballs* by Betsy Byars
   The children in this story feel like pinballs being pushed around from place to place. They stay with a foster-mother and you'll enjoy reading how Carlie comes to help her fellow 'strays'.

3. *Sula* by Lavinia Derwent
   Magnus prefers the company of 'Old Whiskers' to people, but through a strange old hermit called Mr Skinnymalink he finds people can be all right.

Spot the howler

The racecourse has bends and jumps.

Can you say what is odd about this sentence?
   Sailing ships can be fascinating.

To write about

The girl in the story 'Rontu', is alone on an island.
Write a story telling either

    how she got there in the first place

  or

    how she escapes from the island.

Lone Dog

I'm a lean dog, a keen dog, a wild dog and lone,
I'm a rough dog, a tough dog, hunting on my own!
I'm a bad dog, a mad dog, teasing silly sheep;
I love to sit and bay the moon and keep fat souls from sleep.

I'll never be a lap dog, licking dirty feet,
A sleek dog, a meek dog, cringing for my meat.
Not for me the fireside, the well-filled plate,
But shut door and sharp stone and cuff and kick and hate.

Not for me the other dogs, running by my side,
Some have run a short while, but none of them would bide.
O mine is still the lone trail, the hard trail, the best,
Wide wind and wild stars and the hunger of the quest.

                                      Irene McLeod

Searching for missing words

In the passage some words have been missed out.
Can you be sure which words have been missed out?
Sometimes there can be only one answer.
Sometimes there can be several answers for you to think and talk about.
How many words can you find?

Andrew stayed on the main road, instead of going up Becket Road and home. If he went to the top of the hill he would be able to see beyond it, over the roofs, to the office window of the Printing Works, where Mum had probably gone for an hour, to keep the paper-work down. He _____ his way up the hill, against the _____ wind most of the way and then _____ the shelter of a truck. At the _____ he put his bicycle against a lamp-post, _____ the road, and went up the bank _____ the pavement, over the pavement and into a _____ of trees beyond. The street-light shone _____ among the branches of the trees. John _____ once been climbing in these trees, and _____ the office window from one of them; _____ since then he had made an easy _____ up among the branches and up the _____ so that by night he or Andrew _____ easily see whether Mum was at the _____.

From *Cathedral Wednesday* by William Mayne

14

Points of view

Here are a few facts about an incident which takes place one foggy November evening.

U.F.O.

Darkness is falling. Malcolm and Veronica are walking home, having visited their aunt. A huge red object appears in the sky about a hundred metres away and begins to move slowly towards them. The local constable comes round the corner at that point on his bicycle. Constable Brooks sees the object, loses control of his bicycle and ends up in the canal. Malcolm laughs. The object disappears. Constable Brooks looks most annoyed.

Imagine you are

(a) Constable Brooks

or (b) one of the children

or (c) one of the people from outer space in the huge red object.

Could you give an account of the incident from your point of view?

How to use a book

Some books in your classroom or school library are information books.
At the beginning they have a page telling you what is in the book.
It is called a **contents** page.
It can be like this.

CONTENTS		
Chapter 1	Farming	4
Chapter 2	Towns and Villages	12
Chapter 3	Our Rivers	19
Chapter 4	Why we have Mountains and Valleys	27
Chapter 5	Our Plants and Animals	32
Chapter 6	Food from the Sea	42
Chapter 7	Searching for Oil	50
Chapter 8	Country Parks	62
Chapter 9	The Sport of Fishing	74
Chapter 10	Our Weather	80

1. Can you say which chapter you would look up if you wanted to find out more about the topics given below?

Enjoying the countryside	**The Ice Age**
Wildlife	**A bakery**
How much it rains in a year	**Trout**
Transport	**Wheat**

2. Can you think what kind of a book this **contents** page is from?

3. Take any two of the chapter topics in the **contents** page above.
    Can you look them up in a book in your classroom or school library?
    In how many books can you find out about these things?
    Make a list of their titles. Are they different kinds of books?

The sea

The sea is a hungry dog.
Giant and grey.
He rolls on the beach all day.
With his clashing teeth and shaggy jaws
Hour upon hour he gnaws
The rumbling, tumbling stones,
And 'Bones, bones, bones, bones!'
The giant sea-dog moans,
Licking his greasy paws.

And when the night wind roars
And the moon rocks in the stormy cloud,
He bounds to his feet and snuffs and sniffs,
Shaking his wet sides over the cliffs,
And howls and hollos long and loud.

But on quiet days in May or June,
When even the grasses on the dune
Play no more their reedy tune,
With his head between his paws
He lies on the sandy shores,
So quiet, so quiet, he scarcely snores.

      James Reeves

Fact or opinion?

Why do writers mix facts and opinions?
Often they do this because they want you to think the way they do. Sometimes they wish to influence what you do or where you go or what you buy.
Here are some sentences. Some are facts, some are opinions. Sort them out and talk about what the **opinion sentences** wish to make you do or feel or think.

1. People should think more carefully about their lives.
2. The south of France is a magnificent place to go on holiday. (*from a travel brochure*)
3. There are too many cars on our roads, so people should walk to work more often. (*from a book on keep-fit*)
4. Rome and Paris are in different countries.
5. Rome has more interesting places to see than Paris. (*from an Italian Tourist Board magazine*)
6. No household should be without the benefits of radio and television. (*leading manufacturer of hi-fi equipment*)
7. It is now possible to telephone most parts of the world.
8. The Taj Mahal is in India.

Act it out

Ian and his friends were talking about news the postman might bring.
They thought of some things which might be welcome, such as a letter from a friend, a letter about a win in a competition, or an invitation to a party. The children decided to write a sketch about a family at breakfast getting some news by post. They called their sketch 'Postman's Knock'.
Here is how they started.

Postman's Knock

The Jenkins family, Mum, Dad, Lucy and Ben, are at breakfast.

Dad: Pass the sugar, Mum. (*To children*) Stop fighting, you two, or there will be no pocket money this week.
Ben: She kicked me, Dad, it isn't fair. (*There is a knock at the door*) There is the postman (*Rises to his feet*) I'll get it. (*Goes out and returns after a moment with a letter*) It's for you, Dad.
Dad: (*Looks at envelope*) Well, well, it is from the football pools people.
Lucy: Oh Dad, we will be millionaires. Can I have a pony?
Ben: Can I have a new bike, Dad? And a telly of my own? And . . .
Dad: (*Opens the envelope and examines the contents*) Well, I *have* won some money.
Mum: How much, for goodness sake?
Dad: It is slightly less than I earn in three weeks. Goodness, I was getting quite excited myself.
Lucy: But that would buy a pony, you know . . .

What will the other members of the family say now?
Can you think of an interesting way for the sketch to end?
Why not complete 'Postman's Knock' and act it for the rest of your class?

Here is a poem written by a girl called Alice.

Alone on an island

Alone on an island
Except for the things I hear
Listening
To the seagulls screaming
The sea roaring on the rocks
The howling of wild dogs.
Looking
For people
For people long gone
Gazing along the endless beach
Searching the endless blue of the sea
Smelling
The scent of seaweed drying
And the burning wood of the fire.
Thinking
And dreaming alone
Of faraway places
And people.
One day they will return for me.

Did you like Alice's poem?
Write your own poem about being alone on an island.

Reading for the main idea

Phyllis was working on a project about **rescues** and came across his passage in a book.

While out walking along the cliff top enjoying the bracing sea-air, Mr Andrews and his wife both heard shrill cries which they had at first thought to be the sound of wild sea-birds as they wheeled in the air around the rocky coast. Venturing nearer the cliff's edge, they again heard the cries and knew them to be cries for help. But from where? Carefully scanning the area with his field-glasses, Mr Andrews soon saw a young boy clinging to an overhanging rock that jutted out from the cliff face. He raced to fetch help before the lad lost his hold and fell into the crashing waves below. It was not long before some coastguards arrived bringing rope ladders and rescued the boy while the two holiday-makers looked on in silence.

Phyllis made notes of the main ideas in the story. Here is what she wrote:

**Mr and Mrs Andrews walk — cliffs
— hear cries — help.**

Think of the other main ideas in the story. Add them to Phyllis's list so that you have notes of all the main ideas.
Can you use your notes to write your own shortened version of the passage 'Rescue'?

Ideas to write about

1. Imagine you are being sent to a desert island.
   You can take some things with you.
   What would you take? Write about your list.
   Try to give good reasons for your choice.

2. You are the captain of a ship, and you find on an island a lone survivor from a shipwreck.
   Write a report of what happens. Begin like this:

   Captain's Log, January 19th. Sailing towards Australia we noticed smoke coming from an island. At once I ordered the ship to slow down and turn . . .

3. Could you write a description of the sort of island we have been reading about?
   Have sentences about
   the land
   the trees
   the bay
   the buildings you see.
   Say if you would like to live there.

Funny words

What word do you think the artist has drawn in the picture?

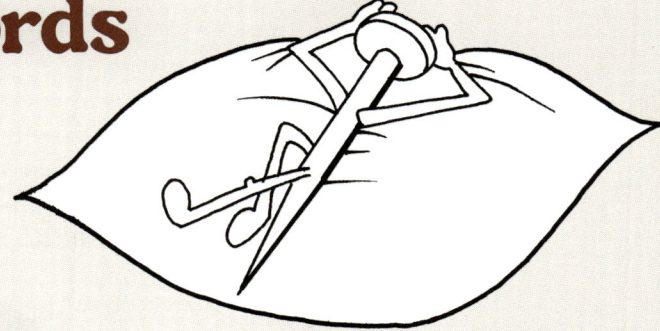

There are lots of words which are funny if you think about them. Talk about how you might make a funny drawing of the word

   doughnut

Can you draw a picture for **doughnut**?

The way words are built

Place names are very interesting. On these pages, some common place names are explained.

Chester
In 55 BC, the Romans invaded the island now known as Britain. Many Roman soldiers came to the island to help govern the people who had been conquered. These soldiers lived in camps. The Latin word for camp was *castra*.

The name Chester is simply that Latin word, which has changed a little.

There are many place names with the ending *-caster*, which is another form of the Latin *castra*. At all of these places there was a Roman camp.

How many place names can you find which end in *-caster* or *-chester*?

Abergavenny
Many place names in Wales begin with *Aber-*, which means a river mouth, or a place where two rivers meet. Abergavenny is the place where the River Gafenni meets the River Usk.

How many place names beginning with *Aber-* can you find?

Devonport

The city of Plymouth in Devon has had a famous history as a seaport. Drake finished a game of bowls on Plymouth Hoe before leading his fleet against the Spanish Armada. The Pilgrim Fathers sailed to America from Plymouth in 1620, and Captain Cook set out for the Pacific in 1772. The Royal Naval Dockyard was already there, in that part of Plymouth which became known as Devonport. Settlers in Australia and New Zealand named ports in Tasmania and Auckland after it, and New Zealand's naval dockyard is at Devonport, halfway round the world from Devonport, England.

What place names can you find which may be connected with Captain Cook's Pacific exploration?

Dunkeld

Many place names start with *Dun-*, which is a Gaelic word, meaning a fort. So, Dun*keld* is the fort of the *Caled*onians, who were one of the tribes living in central Scotland about 1200 years ago.

How many place names beginning with *Dun-* can you find?
How do you think Dunedin got its name?

Can you think of other common beginnings or endings to place names in your country?

Giving instructions

Julia wrote down this list of instructions for something you may recognise.

1. Have ready some change of the right kind.
2. Lift the receiver.
3. Dial the number.
4. Wait for the ringing tone. If no-one answers after a time replace the receiver, and try again later.
5. When someone answers...

Julia has not finished the instructions for making a phone call. Can you add the instructions necessary to finish?

Now think of another action involving a machine. (Some suggestions are given below.)
Write a set of instructions for using the machine, without saying what the machine is.
Suggestions:
    doing washing with an automatic machine
    making a cassette recording
    playing a record
    vacuum cleaning a floor.
Try your instructions on your friends as a puzzle.
Can they guess what the machine is?

Shortened words

Sometimes we do not write a word out in full.
We write only part of it, to save time or space.
If we do that, we put a full stop at the end, to show that some letters have been missed out.

Here are some examples. Write down the words in full.

Oct.	Ltd.
cm.	rd.
Bros.	st.
Thurs.	Mr.
Mrs.	Jan.

Look at a page of any newspaper. How many more examples can you find like those above?

How on earth!

Talk about the strange scene in the picture.
How did it happen?
Why?
Could you write a story about it?

Tyke Tiler and Danny Price are friends who like adventure. In this story Danny has discovered a 'real skellinton'.

This story is taken from a book called *The Turbulent Term of Tyke Tiler* by Gene Kemp.

Dem bones, dem bones

'You've got bones on the brain. That's because you're a bonehead, I suppose...'

'But I tell you it's a real skellinton, Tyke. I tell you where I seen it. Down in the leat. I went there yesterday when you was out. Come on. Come and look. I bet it's somebody what's bin murdered.'

'I got into enough trouble over that marrow bone...'

But Danny had set off along the road as if he was warming up for the fifteen hundred metres. He belted down the bank, where the old city walls stand, that drops down to the river and the leats, the oldest part of the city, Sir says. I soon caught up with him, Crumble at my heels, her ears ruffling out in the wind.

'Which leat are the bones in?'

There are two, Cricklepit and Walter, that cut off from the river below the weir. The leats and the river make an island that's mostly a deserted place. Danny panted:

'By the bridge. Near the warehouses.'

'They weren't there last week.'

'The rain and high water brung 'em out.'

We ran on, past the old, broken water-wheel, hidden in the trees and bushes, where the kingfisher flies sometimes. I've seen him quite a lot lately. I threw a broken brick into the water sluicing through an iron grid. The brown colour had gone but it was still high. Everywhere was quiet. No one comes round here much. Everything's either being knocked down or rotting away; it's a place for secrets and adventures.

Perhaps this was an adventure. Perhaps the bones were the skeleton of a murdered man, or valuable prehistoric remains. We ran through the square where my Gran used to live before it was demolished and on to a little sandstone bridge. Beside it was a wall and a railing and a long drop to the leat. We climbed over and inspected the filthy water.

'There. There it is.'

Danny pointed at what looked like a huge set of teeth decorated with floating strands of green slime. Other bones were scattered around. Crumble made eeking noises on the other side of the wall, so I lifted her over.

'It's lovely, Tyke.'

'It's a sheep, you nutter. It's like that one Martin Kneeshaw brought off the moor and went round showing off.'

'No it's not. It's a man, I tell you. Somebody murdered that man and chucked his body in here and he mouldered and mouldered away till he was that skellinton.'

'It's a sheep . . .'

He took no notice.

'We'll be on telly. Danny Price and Tyke Tiler found a murdered skellinton. Do you think there'll be a reward?' Crumble ran up and down the muddy bank, taking great interest in the bones as well. I didn't think she would leap off the bank, though, as it was a long way down to the water.

'You must know it's a sheep, Danny...' but he wasn't listening. His face was white and his eyes glittered. Completely nutty... mad as a snake... absolutely bonkers.

'Get it for me, Tyke.'

'What?'

'Get it for me. I want it.'

I looked at the dirty, scummy water. This leat always got choked up, yet in the centre the current ran fast and fierce. Danny gazed at the bones as if they were the Crown Jewels.

'My Mum will wallop me if I get mucky again. She said so.'

'I want them bones.'

'Get 'em, then.'

'It's too steep for me.'

'Then it's too steep for me, too!'

'But you're clever. You can do anything.'

'Gee t'anks. For nothing.'

'If I take it to school I'll get some house points.'

'I thought you wanted to be famous. You won't get on the telly with sheep's teeth and house points. Make up your mind.'

'If it's a murdered man's skellinton, then I'll go on the telly and be famous, and if it's a sheep's I'll get some house points.'

He was starting to talk faster and faster and suddenly I thought maybe he'd gone completely bonkers, and I'd better humour him, so I said what about some chips because I'm starving and I could fix him up with some fossils to take to school instead.

He wasn't listening.

'Get them bones for me, Tyke.'

'I don't want to . . .' and then I stopped. You can't get through to Danny when he's got an idea in his head, for there's only room for one at a time. I studied the water down below. The bottom was covered with broken bricks over which lay tins, bits of metal, sticks and wire, and the bones veiled in their green slime drifting and weaving in the current. It looked pretty deep. I wasn't likely to get drowned here — not like the river — but it looked cold and unfriendly. I thought of me Mum, and I looked at Danny still gazing at the bones and talking. Holding on to a tree root I lowered myself into the mucky, muddy, slimy water. I didn't seem worth taking my shoes and socks off as my trousers would get soaked anyway. Anyway I'd got my doom feeling by now. My doom feeling is when I know I'm slap bang in the middle of something that

will lead to trouble, but I can't stop doing it all the same. I could hear my Gran saying:

'You might as well be hung for a sheep as a lamb.'

She used to say a lot of things like that.

Danny danced about on the edge of the bank.

'That's it, Tyke. You've nearly got 'em.'

There was a slithering noise, and an enormous splash. A piece of weed hit me on the nose and I was wet all over. Crumble had arrived to help. She lifted her nose in the air and started to swim, back legs kicking hard. She flurried all the water and I lost the bones. I couldn't see a thing.

'You stupid fool of a dog, get out,' I yelled. She swam round and round me, nose in the air. The water was icy even through shoes, socks and trousers. I reached into the mud and found the bones.

'It's the teethy ones I want," Danny jumped up and down.

'It stinks!'

It was slimily, horribly soft to the touch as well, a yellow jawbone with long teeth. I moved to the bank to hand it up to Danny. Crumble tried

to follow this delightful pong and, getting to the bank, snapped at the teeth, then fell back into the water again.

'And the rest,' Danny roared, hopping, by now.

I got the rest. They felt really horrible. They smelt worse.

Danny cradled them in his arms, making little humming noises.

'I got a bag,' he said, bringing one out of his pocket. He put the bones in it and gathered it to his chest. The bag went soggy. Crumble and I started to climb the bank. Danny went over the wall.

'Hey! Gimme a hand!'

He managed to remember me for a moment and stretched out a mitt, but the bank was so churned up with all his leaping about that he suddenly slipped, and fell flat on his back, bones clasped to his chest.

Down I crashed on to the slimy stones in that stinking leat. Crumble joined me, licking my face as I tried to get to my feet. Danny Price sat on the bank, laughing like a drain.

Wild with fury, I travelled up that bank at a thousand miles per hour, dragging Crumble by her collar.

'I'm gonna exterminate you, and bury you with your rotten old bones!'

I've got twice his speed, but sopping wet trousers and squelching shoes don't help. Crumble kept running in and out of my legs. I gave up and headed for home instead.

Linda Stoatway watched from her doorway.

'You a mermaid, eh, Tyke?' she giggled and collapsed on Lorraine Fairchild standing behind her.

I tried to get in without being seen, through the back door and up to the bathroom, as quiet as a mouse with rubber boots on. Crumble I left outside to dry off, I hoped.

Only at that moment me Mum had just taken Aunt Marge to view our new posh lilac bath. Aunt Marge needn't have screamed as loud as she did. I've never liked her. Afterwards Mum said it was that scream just as much as the sight of me soaked in slime that upset her.

Danny got his house points but after a day Sir said he couldn't bear the smell any longer and would we take the bones away. We did.

We took them to the leat and threw them in. I stopped Crumble from jumping in after them.

'I think them teeth are grinning at us,' said Danny.

'I wouldn't be at all surprised,' I replied.

Dad says he hates the new lilac bath and Mum must've been mad to choose such a colour.

To think and talk about

A 1. How can you tell that Danny is getting excited? Is there more than one clue?

2. 'But you're clever. You can do anything,' says Danny. Do you think Danny really means what he says?

3. Did Danny really want the bones or did he just want to see if Tyke would go for them? What do you think?

4. Can you spot any clues in the story which suggest whether Tyke Tiler is a boy or a girl?

B 1. Does Tyke go after the bones simply to please Danny or is there some other reason?

2. Do you think Tyke lives in a town or a city? Would you like to live there? Give some reasons for your answers.

3. Tyke says 'My Mum will wallop me if I get mucky again. She said so.' What other adventures do you think the two have been up to?

4. What do you imagine the teacher at school said when presented with the bones?

C 1. If you were Tyke Tiler what would you have done in this situation?

2. What do you think the police would say if you arrived at the station with a 'skellinton'?

3. From the information in the story how would you describe Tyke Tiler?

4. 'Danny Price sat on the bank laughing like a drain.' What sort of a person is Danny Price?

More books to read

1. *Wood Street Books* by Mabel E. Allan
   This is a popular series of books. Why not start with *The Wood Street Secret*? This is the story of how Cherry and her brother Ben make friends with five other local children.

2. *Latchkey Children* by Eric Allen
   Bill and Ben, Froggy, Goggles, Etty and Duke Ellington Binns try to save a special tree from being replaced by a concrete engine. True to life adventures you'll be amused to read about.

3. *A Hundred Million Francs* by Paul Berna
   This book was voted best book of its year by French boys and girls and you will probably understand why if you read about this gang of children who get on the scent of thieves because of an old battered toy horse.

To write about

One evening Danny and Tyke are walking near an old ruin. Danny sees a light hovering and flickering inside. He immediately concludes it's an Unidentified Flying Object and people from another planet are about to invade earth.

Write the story of what Danny and Tyke do.
Mention the people they tell.
What does the light turn out to be?

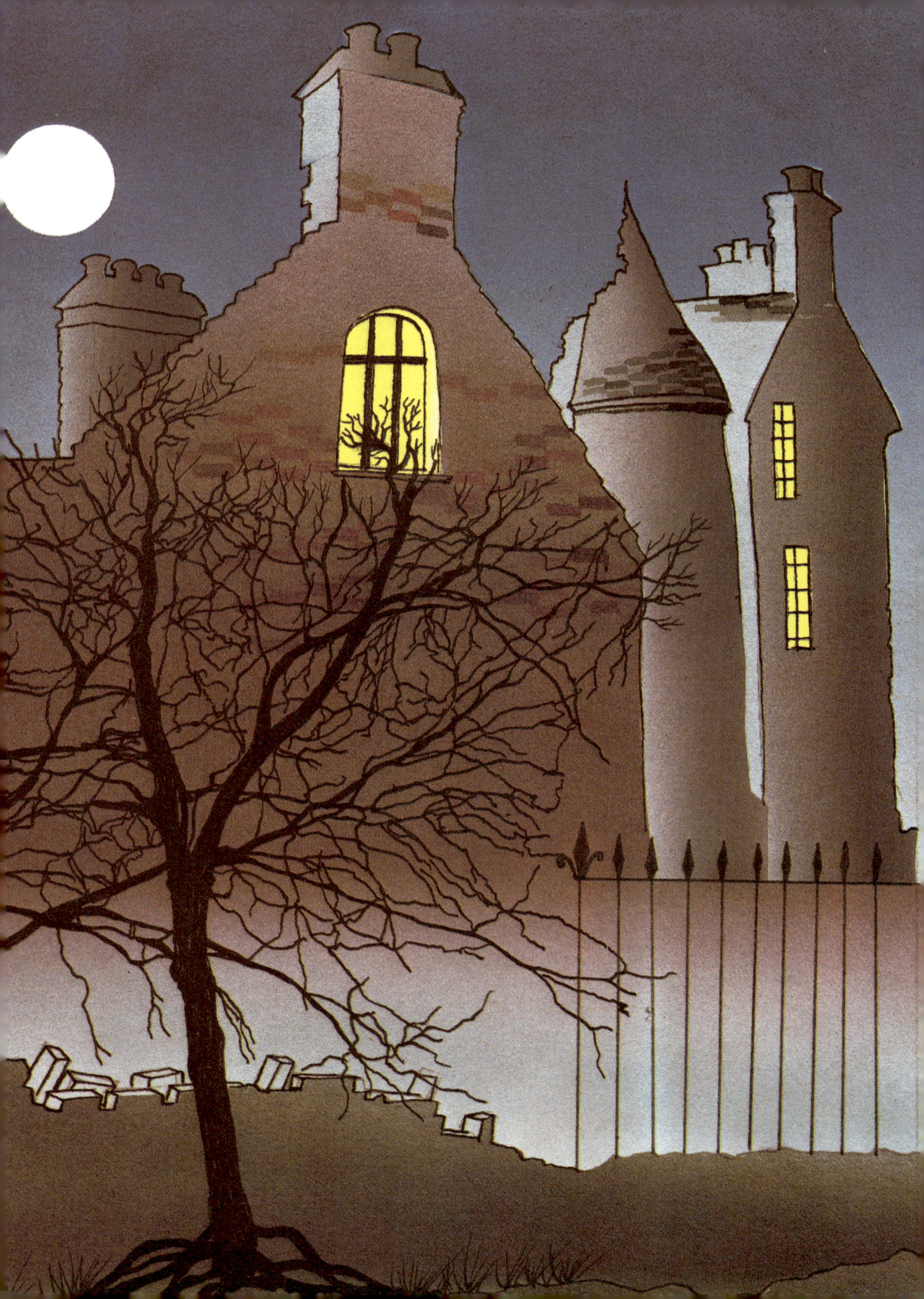

First day at school

A millionbillionwillion miles from home
Waiting for the bell to go. (To go where?)
Why are they all so big, other children?
So noisy? So much at home they
must have been born in uniform
Lived all their lives in playgrounds
Spent the years inventing games
that don't let me in. Games
that are rough, that swallow you up.

And the railings.
All around, the railings.
Are they to keep out wolves and monsters?
Things that carry off and eat children?
Things you don't take sweets from?
Perhaps they're to stop us getting out
Running away from the lessins. Lessin.
What does a lessin look like?
Sounds small and slimy.
They keep them in glassrooms.
Whole rooms made out of glass. Imagine.

I wish I could remember my name
Mummy said it would come in useful.
Like wellies. When there's puddles.
Yellowwellies. I wish she was here.
I think my name is sewn on somewhere
Perhaps the teacher will read it for me.
Tea-cher. The one who makes the tea.

                                       Roger McGough

Searching for missing words

In the passage some words have been missed out.
Can you be sure which words have been missed out?
Sometimes there can be only one answer.
Sometimes there can be several answers for you to think and talk about.
How many words can you find?

That night the general ordered a thousand huge earthenware jars to be placed around the besieged city. Inside each jar was one soldier armed to the teeth. The rest of the Egyptian army then picked up their _arms_ and baggage, cleared out of the _camp_ and beat a retreat. The besieged townspeople _ran_ to the city walls and no longer _saw_ any Egyptians. They did see the earthenware _jars_ and shouted:

   'Good. The olive harvest is _ready/here_. Just what we need.'

   A hundred carriages _were_ needed to carry the jars into the _city_. That night the Egyptian soldiers broke out _of_ their jars, opened the gates of the _city_ and set fire to it. The Pharaoh _attacked_ with all his troops. The outcome of the _battle_ was victory, big celebrations and fireworks.

   General Tuttia _was_ the only one who did not seem _pleased/happy_ about the victory:

   'What's wrong?' asked the _Pharaoh_. 'I've given you the most distinguished medals _in_ the land, a first-class pension and one _1000_ horses — one for each jar. What more could you possibly want?'

From *Tales Told by a Machine* by Gianni Rodari

Points of view

The Wedding

It was ten o'clock on Saturday morning — the day my elder brother Frank was getting married. I was all ready and dressed in my bridesmaid's outfit, a long yellow dress that I kept tripping over. Tom, my other brother, was sulking in his best clothes, while Mum checked her hat in the mirror for the tenth time. The only one we were waiting for was Dad. He came in stiffly in his only suit that he saved for weddings and funerals. He was just bending down to tie up his shoe lace when rip — his jacket split down the back. Then the doorbell rang, the wedding car had arrived.

Imagine you are

    (a) Frank
or (b) Dad
or (c) the author.

Could you tell or write an account of the incident from your point of view?

Sort it out

1. The sentences below go together to make a story, but they are in the wrong order. Can you write them in the correct order?

    (a) It was not yet nine o'clock in the morning.

    (b) Kano and Jebda set off and were soon making good progress up a steep ascent.

    (c) At any rate he landed badly and quite clearly had broken an ankle.

    (d) It was not long before Jebda was rescued and taken to hospital.

    (e) Perhaps it was overconfidence that made Jebda jump a small mound of stones.

    (f) The day dawned bright and clear and looked perfect for hill walking.

    (g) Kano, having made his friend as comfortable as possible, returned to base.

2. These sentences make a set of instructions for getting from Louise's school to her home. Can you put them in the right order?

    (a) Halfway down Napier Terrace, turn left into Gasworks Lane.

    (b) Take the third turning, which is Napier Terrace.

    (c) At the corner of the Gasworks site, turn left.

    (d) On leaving school, turn left and walk down Larch Drive to the traffic lights.

    (e) At the lights, cross straight over and turn right down Napier Road.

    (f) My house is in the third block on the left, but you have to ring the bell at the bottom of the stair.

Fact or opinion?

Here is part of a conversation which is made up of a number of facts and opinions.

Billy is trying to persuade Sandra to join a local club.
   'You should come along one evening — it's great! We've got table tennis, badminton, volleyball, depending on what you prefer.'
   'Bet you end up playing indoor football most weeks,' interrupted Sandra.
   'Sometimes — but not always,' continued Billy. 'If more girls came along they could have more of a say.'
   'I prefer to know exactly what's going to happen before I go. That way I won't be disappointed,' said Sandra.
   'Look,' said Billy, 'I'll tell you what — come along on Monday night and give it a try. It's the large hall next to the library and we get the use of the coffee bar.'
   'Well, all right,' replied Sandra. 'I'll come along. But remember ... I don't like wild games — so no football!'

Can you write down all the **opinions** you can spot?
Remember facts are those which can be definitely proved.
Opinions are to do with what someone thinks or feels.

Ideas to write about

1. Tyke seems to get into situations that lead to trouble. Tyke thinks of the 'doom feeling'.
   'My doom feeling is when I know I'm slap bang in the middle of something that will lead to trouble, but I can't stop doing it all the same.'
   Can you write about a situation where you are landed 'slap bang in the middle of something' and decide you may as well 'be hung for sheep as a lamb'?

2. Read over the first part of the story where the author describes the place where the action is to take place.
   Think of a spot you know and go to often.
   Describe it as carefully as you can.
   Have sentences about
      the buildings
      the landscape
      the river or hills or sea.
   Finish your description by writing a few sentences which tell how you feel about this well known spot.

3. Imagine that you are either Aunt Marge or Tyke's father. Write about what happens when Tyke is discovered all covered in slime.

Late home

I looked up — the sun had gone down
Though it was there a minute before
And the light had grown terribly thin
And no one played by the shore
Of the lake, now empty, and still;
And I heard the park-keepers shout
As they cycled the paths . . .
'Closing, closing . . . everyone out . . .'

Then I panicked and started to run,
Leaving all of my friends behind
(I could hear their cries in the bushes —
It was me they were trying to find)
But they had the burn and the minnows,
The rope, the slide, the shrubbery track,
And the trees where a thrush was singing,
And I had the long road back —

The road that led, empty and straight,
Down under the tall grey flats
Where the lights were on, and the tellies,
And old ladies were putting out cats:
I ran past them, without looking round
As though I'd committed a crime:
At six they'd said 'Just half an hour'
And *now* — oh, what was the time?

How could it have gone already?
Something must be, it *must* be, wrong —
I've only just come out — and why
Does getting back take me so long?
I can't be late — or if I am,
It's the fault of the sun or the moon.
When the dentist's takes an eternity,
How are happy things over so soon?

So I stopped and asked, 'Please mister...'
And his left wrist came slowly round
And he peered at his watch and shook it
And said 'Blast, it's never been wound up.'
But the next man hauled his watch up,
Like a lead sinker on a line,
Clicked open the front, and boomed out,
'Right now, child, it's five to nine'.

There's a great big gap in between
The way things are, the way things seem,
And I dropped down it then, like you do
When you shoot back to life from a dream.
I stood there and muttered 'It can't be —
His watch must be wrong' — then, aghast —
'This time, I'll *really* be for it.
If it isn't a whole two hours fast.'

But I got my legs going again
And ran, gulping in red-hot air,
Through back-streets where no one knew me,
Till I came out in the Town Square.
But when I looked at the shining face
And I heard the cheerful chimes
Of the Town Hall clock — then every hope
Drained away, as it struck nine times.

Two hours late . . . two hours late —
Perhaps they've called out the police
Two hours late . . . who, all in a line,
Are combing the waste ground, piece by piece;
While *they* all stand in our window
Anxious and angry and, when I'm seen,
Ready to frown and shout 'There he is',
'Come here you!', and 'Where's the child been?'

When I come round the corner and see them,
I'll limp, as though I'd a sprain,
Then whimper 'I didn't mean it' and
'I'll never ever go out, again . . .
How can I know that time's up,
When I'm enjoying myself such a lot?
I'm sorry — won't you take me back in?
Are you glad to see me, or not?'

. . . But later in bed, as I lay there
In the extraordinary light —
Filtering through the half-drawn curtain —
Of that silvery spellbound night,
I wondered just what *had* happened
To Time, for three hours in June:
If all of my life is as happy —
Will it all be over as soon?

                                        Brian Lee

Act it out

Jackie and her friends were talking about what they thought they would do in certain situations, such as a fire, a shipwreck, and the like.
But then someone said: 'What would you do if you were walking in the woods and you found human bones?'
Here is some of what the children said.

Jackie: I'd get someone to stay on the scene and go for help.
Paul: I'd go for the police.
Laurie: You'd look a right fool if they were sheep's bones. They'd probably lock you up.

What do you think *you* would do?
Perhaps you could make a short play about this idea.
Try to give it a **beginning** (finding the bones)
a **middle** (what you do)
an **end** (what happens)
Who will be in the play?
Why not act the play for your friends?

Spot the howler

Haystacks can be seen driving through the countryside.

Can you say what is wrong with this sentence?

The runaway car fell into the river and it stopped moving.

Reading for the main idea

Peter was working on a project about **elephants** and came across this passage in a book.

The largest of India's animals is the elephant. Its most noticeable features are its trunk and tusks, the latter being often sought after for making ivory goods. The trunk is a wonderful limb resembling a nose and an arm, with which it is able to pick up the smallest thing or suck up grain or maize. It uses its trunk to tear foliage from the trees to eat or to spray its huge body with water from the river in order to cool itself down. In certain forest areas it is trained to roll and stack logs using its tusks to steady each log. The bull elephant will make use of his long fearsome tusks when protecting his domain from other invading elephants who challenge his leadership. This magnificent creature can live for more than a century in the wild. Elephants live in herds, each member being loyal to every other member.

Peter made notes of the main ideas in the story. Here is what he wrote:

— **elephant largest animal — India**
— **trunk and tusks most important.**

Think of the other main ideas in the story. Add them to Peter's list so that you have all the main ideas.
Can you use your notes to write a shortened version of the passage — 'The Elephant'?

To write about

Look at what is happening in this picture.
Can you write about what Dad does and says as he watches the dog burying his teeth?

Using a dictionary

Use your dictionary to answer these quesions by looking up the word which is in bold type in each sentence.

1. Would you write someone else's **autobiography?** Why?
2. Would you be likely to see a **blond** girl? Why?
3. Would you recover quickly from a **chronic** illness?
4. If you **exaggerate** something, how much of the truth have you told?
5. If you were **immersed** in the swimming pool, how much of you would be under water?
6. If you cut down the trees surrounding a house, would that **seclude** it? Why?
7. Why could you not read a page which had been **obliterated**?
8. Would you be surprised to read your own **obituary**? Why?
9. How would you like to have your illness treated by a **quack**? Why?
10. If you had a **smattering** of Russian, how well could you speak the language?

The way words are built

First Names

Do you know what your first name means? Some are easy to understand like these:

      Joy   **June**   **Rose**   **Victor**

Many first names have no obvious meaning, but nearly all mean something.

Here are some common first names with their possible meanings, and the language from which they come.

Abigail	*father rejoiced*	Hebrew
Adam	*man*	Hebrew
Andrew	*manly*	Greek
Bernard	*bear-head*	German
Brenda	*a sword*	Norse
Clare	*bright*	Latin
David	*beloved*	Hebrew
Deborah	*bee*	Hebrew
Diana	*goddess*	Latin
Dolores	*sorrows*	Spanish
Edith	*rich war*	Old English
Francis	*French*	French
Gavin	*white hawk*	Welsh
George	*farmer*	Greek
Helen	*bright*	Greek
James	*follower*	from Latin Jacob
Jennifer	*white wave*	Welsh
Lewis	*famous warrior*	German
Margaret	*pearl*	Greek
Norman	*Northman*	German
Patrick	*nobleman*	Latin
Rachel	*ewe*	Hebrew
Stella	*star*	Latin
Stephen	*crown*	Greek

If you would like to find out more about your name, most good dictionaries have a section at the back on first names.

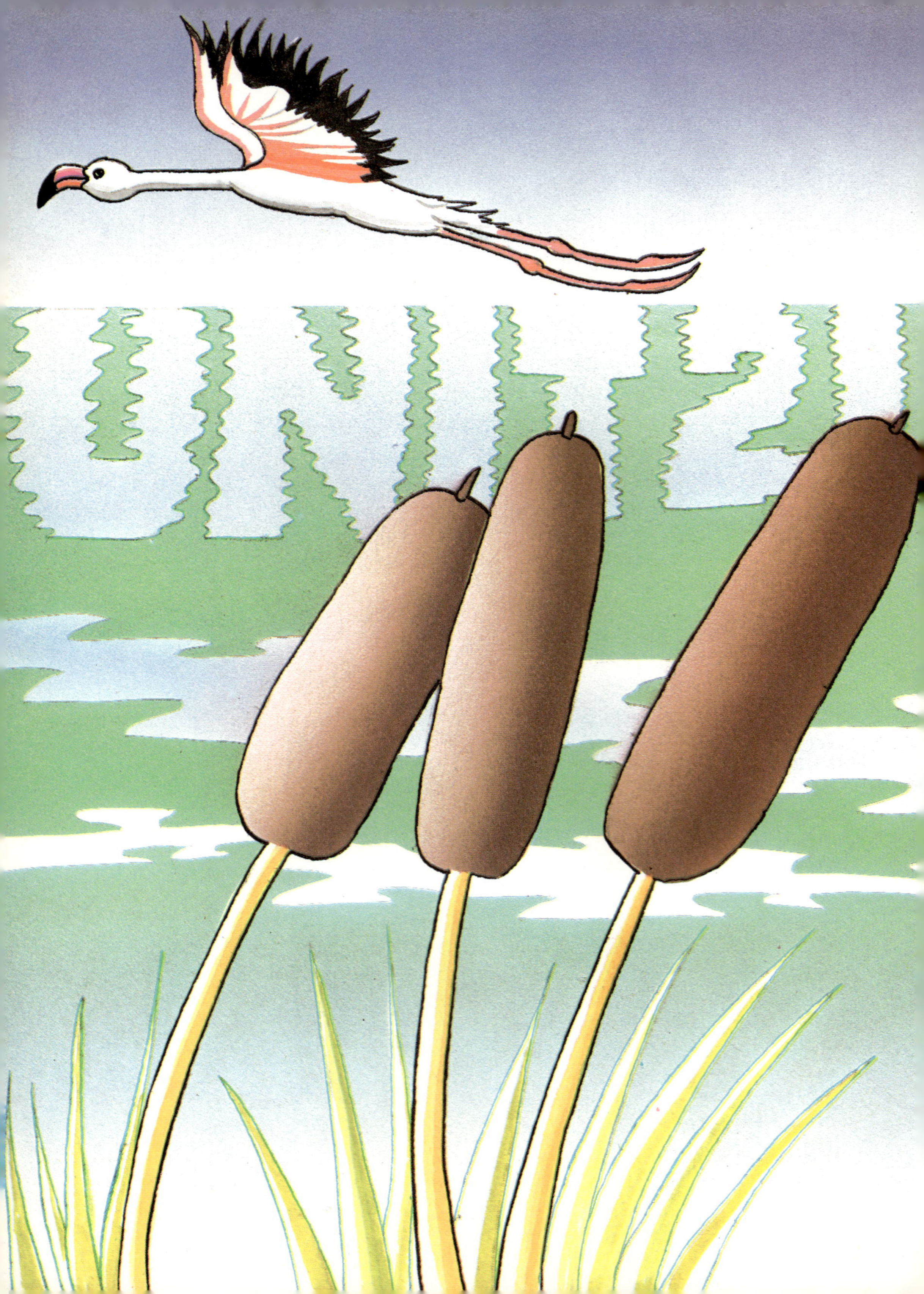

As two boys, Apu and Khoka, approach the shore in their canoe they wonder if, at last, they have found the island of Kukuri Mukuri which is their home.

This story is taken from a book called *The Night the Water Came* by Clive King.

Journey's End

We drifted slowly towards the shore.

Khoka spoke: 'If this isn't Kukuri Mukuri, where is it?'

'I don't know,' I said. 'I suppose we can ask. Do you think they'll feed us here?'

'They'd better,' he said. 'I'm starving again.'

We paddled towards a landing place. There were two tall soldiers standing there. They waited until we had beached the boat, then one of them said jokingly, 'And what's brought you here?'

Questions again. What had brought us there? I was tired and disappointed and didn't know the right answer. The easiest thing seemed to be to tell the truth. I said: 'A rickshaw and a rowing-boat and a cargo boat and two country boats and a bus and a buffalo cart and this canoe. And the tide.'

The soldier laughed, but not very pleasantly, and said, 'Then you'd better go back.'

I felt very weak. 'I can't,' I said.

'Why not?'

'The tide's going the wrong way.'

The soldier spoke with the other soldier in a manner I couldn't follow. They seemed to be talking about the water. Then he turned to me and said, 'You'll have to go back on the next tide.'

'We're hungry,' Khoka said. 'Haven't you any food for us?'

'You'll have to ask Mr Enamel,' said the soldier.

I asked who Mr Enamel was and the soldier said he was the Relief Officer. We left the boat on the beach and they took us to a tent. I was used to finding tents all over the islands and of course the buildings we'd seen were more tents. In the tent were tables and chairs, and the tables were stacked with piles of paper. There was a man sitting on a chair behind one of these piles and I could hardly see his head over the top. He peered over at me through his spectacles. His eyes were neither kind nor unkind, just worried, but my heart sank. I knew it was questions again. They started.

'Name?'

'Apu, or Anisuzzaman.'

'Father's name?'

'Bashir.'

'Living?'

'No.'

'Guardian?'

'Ahmed son of Kabir. But he's dead too.'

'Then he can't be your guardian, can he?' I was surprised that Mr Enamel could speak a whole sentence, and I didn't know what to say. I preferred the short questions, they were less muddling. A short question came.

'Home?'

Home? Home! Did people have homes? Did I have a home? What was a home? Was it a tent? A *char* in the middle of the water? A mudbank in the middle of the night? A school dormitory? A hotel? A shack made of a broken packing case? A tree floating in a cyclone? My mind spun as I tried to think of the right answer. It was funny, the roof of the tent was spinning too. I felt very strange and the ground was coming up to meet me . . .

I slowly woke up and opened my eyes to see a strange blue light all round me and a white figure standing beside me. Was I in paradise with an angel? No, it was a blue tent with the sunlight shining through the cloth and the figure was a nurse. She asked me how I was, in my own language, then went and fetched a glass from the top of a packing case and offered it to me. It was that watery powdery milk again, but I was glad to drink it.

I said, 'What happened and where am I?' I remember thinking even then it was better to ask questions than answer them. The nurse smiled and told me I had fainted and I was in the hospital tent. Then I asked where Khoka was. She pointed across the tent and I saw Khoka, lying like myself on a mattress on the ground, grinning at me.

When the nurse went out Khoka said, 'I fainted too. It seemed the only way to stop them asking questions. At least I lay with my eyes shut while they talked about us. Seems we can't stay on the island unless we're written on the paper and we can't be written on the paper unless we've got permission to stay on the island.'

I lay back on my mattress and felt very tired, but Khoka went on: 'Don't worry. We're on the hospital list now. So don't be in too much of a hurry to get well.'

I looked up at the blue roof. My mind told me I ought to be thinking of moving on, yet I couldn't imagine going any further. In spite of the strange surroundings I had an odd feeling of being at my journey's end — even a feeling of being at home, thought there seemed to be no reason for it.

I finished my glass of milk but I was still hungry and I said so to Khoka.

'Why don't you ask for some food then?' Khoka said. 'I've had some — real rice and hot chillies. That's what made me want to stay.'

The nurse came back and I asked for some food. She said the doctor was on the other side of the island and she didn't know whether I ought to have anything. I told her I'd die of starvation if she didn't feed me, so she began opening a tin. When I saw the grey powder in it I said I needed real food. She knew what I meant and eventually fetched me a plate of rice, vegetables and spices. I shovelled it into my mouth with my fingers and felt that I was myself again.

After the meal I went outside the tent to rinse my hands at a water bucket that stood there, and then sat in the sun watching the people pass by towards the place where food was being given out. A little girl wrapped in a green cloth went past with a big empty pot on her head. She looked at me, smiled shyly and said, 'Hullo, Apu!'

'Hullo, Alia!' I said in reply. Perhaps I hadn't really recovered from my faint. At first I didn't feel at all surprised to recognise one of my little cousins. Then I jumped up and called her back. She stopped and turned round.

'Alia! What are you doing here?' I asked.

'Getting food,' she replied, and was about to walk on.

'But how did you get here?'

'In the boat,' she said. It was my turn to be asking silly questions and getting odd answers.

'What boat? Who with? Why did you come to this place?' I asked. And now it was Alia who was getting confused and tongue-tied. She was only a young girl, younger than me, and not very bright.

'I came back with Mother and Father and the uncles and aunties,' she said. Then she drew the end of her green dress over her head, as even the little girls do when they are shy and confused, and she moved off quickly and joined the crowd that was waiting for food. I was too astonished to follow her before she mixed with the crowd, and once she was among them I couldn't go around looking under all the green head-dresses. It's not a thing a boy can do.

She had said, 'I came back.' What could that mean? And what uncles and aunties was she talking about? One of them could be my guardian, uncle Ahmed, and if I could find him I might — well, I might be able to make myself a real person again, properly written down on paper, instead of a bit of water-weed floating around with the tide. That's what I felt like.

I decided I'd go back and try Mr Enamel again. I'd ask *him* questions this time. I walked to the office tent, paused at the door, and asked, 'May I enter?' as I'd been taught to do at school.

Mr Enamel's head and spectacles bobbed up over his piles of papers.

'What do you want?' he asked.

'Where's my uncle Ahmed?' I asked.

Mr Enamel heaved a deep sigh which blew a cloud of dust off the top of the papers.

'Didn't I see you this morning?' he asked.

'Yes,' I said. He took a paper from the top of a pile and looked at it.

'You're Apu, otherwise known as Anisuzzamann, son of Bashir?'

'Yes.'

'And you're an orphan, in the care of Ahmed son of Kabir?'

'Yes.'

'This morning you said that Ahmed son of Kabir was dead.'

'Yes.'

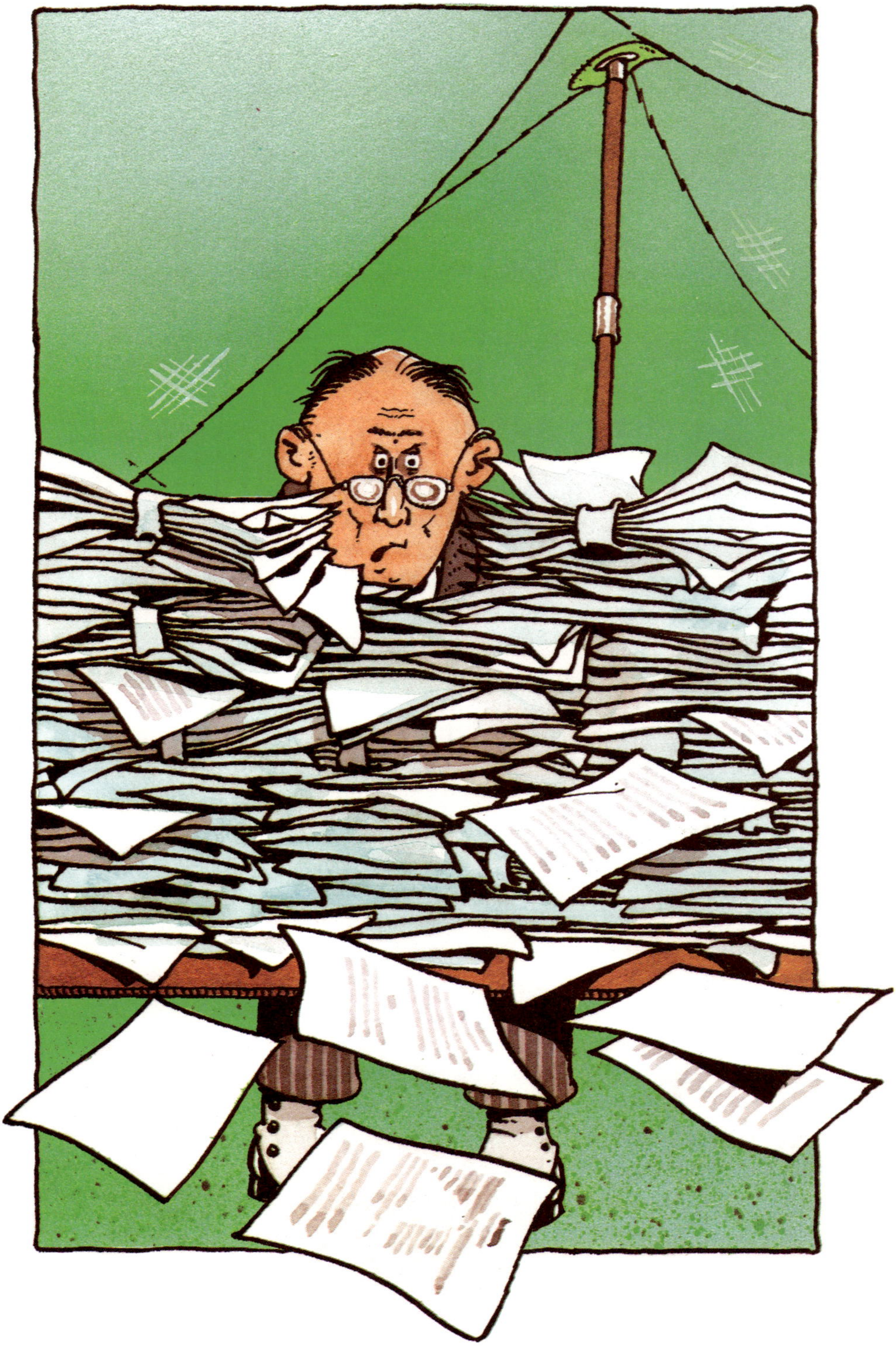

'And now you want to know where he is?'

'Yes, I've been told he is alive.'

The Relief Officer sighed again, hard enough to send a slip of paper floating off the table. I crawled under it, picked up the paper and handed it back.

'I have to inform you,' continued Mr Enamel, 'that I have here a statement from Ahmed son of Kabir, signed with his thumb-print and dated three days ago, certifying that Apu son of Bashir is dead.'

'Oh,' I said. I wasn't sure I understood.

'In other words your uncle has stated that you're dead and you have stated that he's dead.'

'I see.' I was getting confused again.

'Someone's telling lies round here,' said the Relief Officer sternly. 'Either he's dead or you're dead. Which is it?'

I was really muddled now. But of course I'd been brought up to believe that grown-ups were always right. I hung my head and said meekly, 'It must be me that's dead, sir.'

The Relief Officer looked relieved and made a note on the paper. 'I'm glad you admit it,' he said, smoothing back his smooth hair. 'With the Governor coming tomorrow everything's got to be cut and dried.' I supposed he was talking about the rice crop — cutting and drying was something I understood. I knew that was important and felt rather ashamed of myself for going around wasting this man's time. As I walked rather sadly out of the tent I turned and saw him looking at me with a puzzled expression on his face. I thought I'd risk one more question.

'If uncle Ahmed's alive, sir, where is he living?'

'In his *bari*, of course,' came the answer from behind the pile of papers.

'I see. Thank you, sir,' I said. But I didn't see.

I wandered off round the other tents of the camp. There was a small crowd of island people round the entrance to a dark green tent, so I joined them and peered in. Inside there was one of our people, an old man with white hair, sitting on a box with his back to me, and facing a lot of strangers. There were some city people like Mr Enamel; a small round man with dark hair and a white pyjama but who didn't seem to be one of our people; a very tall man with jute hair cut very short; a man in blue trousers with a lot of black hair and beard; a person in trousers with hair that looked as if a bird had tried to make a nest out of jute, who I decided was a woman; a very thin person with a lot of red hair standing on end who I decided was a man; a very large person in a long white dress who must have been a man because he had a beard. I can't remember how many there were altogether or exactly what they looked like but it was no wonder the island people gathered round to stare at the odd collection. I nudged one of the crowd and asked if the old man was giving them a lesson, but he didn't seem to be too sure who was telling who what.

The old man got up and turned to go. It was my uncle! Not my uncle Ahmed who looked after me but another uncle who had been headman on our island. I greeted him excitedly and he looked at me without much surprise.

'What are you doing here, Uncle?' I asked.

'I'm chalking out a plan,' he replied with dignity, and walked on.

'Uncle, how can I get food and clothes?'

'That is easy, my boy. Our good friends are giving us not only food and clothes but schools and teachers and boats and I think aeroplanes as well.'

'But they say my name isn't on the paper.'

'Ah, of course your name must be on the paper. After that it's easy.'

'Can you put my name on the paper, Uncle?'

'My dear child, you know I can't write. But there are plenty of people who can. Go to Mr Enamel and tell him I sent you.' And he walked off in procession with the strangers, talking of jetties and airstrips.

There seemed to be nothing else to do but go back to Mr Enamel. I paused and said, 'May I enter?'

His eyes bobbed up and looked at me. 'What do you want?' he asked.

'I want to get on the paper.'

'Oh, it's you again,' he said. 'You'll have to go back where you came from. Where do you come from?'

'I come from Kukuri Mukuri Char,' I said.

'Well, you'll have to go back there.' He disappeared behind his papers. I wandered towards the door. Before I got there he stopped me.

'Where did you say you came from?' he demanded.

'Kukuri Mukuri Char.'

'Impossible,' he said.

I stood still for a bit, but I couldn't let it go at that. I asked, 'Why is it impossible, sir?'

'Because this is Kukuri Mukuri Char,' he said flatly.

I thought about this for a bit. Then I said respectfully, 'I beg your pardon, sir, that *that* is impossible.'

'Why is it impossible?' he asked crossly.

'Because I come from there and it's not like this.'

He got quite angry. 'First you say you're dead. Now you say you come from Kukuri Mukuri Char when in fact you've come *to* Kukuri Mukuri Char. You're wasting my time.'

I went out feeling sad and more muddled than ever. Not only was I dead and with nowhere to go, but I hadn't even come from the place I'd come from.

I was glad to meet Khoka outside the tent. He looked at me and said, 'What's the matter? Have you seen a ghost?'

'No,' I answered. 'But I think I *am* one.' I told him what the Relief Officer had said to me. He thumped me on the back and said, 'Don't worry about him! All these people who can read and write are the same. It gets them muddled. Come and meet these people I've met. They say I can join their family. Perhaps they'll take you as well.'

It was late in the evening as I followed him across the fields, over a creek by a new bamboo bridge and towards a cluster of *bari* huts on a mound. The red sun was going down over the paddy and our long shadows stretched towards a clump of trees with fresh green leaves shining on the battered branches. I saw that what I'd thought to be huts were in fact tents. But if they had been huts, and if there had been more trees, and more branches on the trees that were standing, it would have looked quite like my old *bari*. Again I had that strange peaceful feeling of coming home. I felt it but I didn't of course believe it.

I felt shy of going to this strange family and asking if I could join them. Khoka said there was nothing to be afraid of. They'd lost some of their own people and were glad to adopt him. But then Khoka was quite shameless, and used to pushing himself where he mightn't be wanted.

I hung back outside the *bari* and told him to go ahead and speak for me. The whole place reminded me so much of my old home that I was almost in tears again. Khoka told me not to be so soft, but he agreed to go in and ask.

He was quite a long time gone. I sat at the bottom of the *bari* mound and watched the sun dip behind the trees. Khoka came out, looking embarrassed.

'They say they can only take one boy of my age, in place of one who disappeared. They'll pretend I'm him. They say they'll get me on the papers, but they can't do it twice. Come on in though. They'll give you a bed for the night, I'm sure.'

I thought I'd better go back to the hospital tent, where at least I was on a list. I didn't want just another bed for the night. But Khoka persuaded me and dragged me up the mound and round the tents, which stood with their backs to the outside world just as the huts had done.

Sitting in front of the tent was my uncle Ahmed.

To think and talk about

A 1. What do you think is happening on the island at the start of the story?

2. Apart from hunger why do you think Apu and Khoka fainted?

3. From your reading of the story in what ways would you say Apu and Khoka are different from each other?

4. Why does Apu admit to being dead when he is obviously alive?
   Why is Mr Enamel relieved at his answer?

B 1. Why do you think Apu prefers to ask questions rather than be asked?

2. Why do you think Apu and his family left the island in the first place?

3. What would you like or dislike about Mr Enamel's job?

4. At the end of the story Apu finds his uncle. What will now happen to him? What about Khoka?

C 1. You arrive on this island. At once you are told you must leave unless you are 'on the list'. How would you feel in this situation?

2. Towards the end of the story the writer says to himself 'Again I had that strange peaceful feeling of coming home. I felt it but I didn't, of course, believe it.' Imagine you had been lost for many days or weeks. How would you describe your feelings on reaching home?

3. At times in the story Apu is almost impertinent to adults. Yet on another occasion he will admit to being dead. How would you descibe Apu?

4. Think of the events and the people in the story. Would you like to live on this island? Give reasons for your answer.

More books to read

1. *House of Sixty Fathers* by Meindert DeJong
   This story is about the courage of Tren Pao who is separated by war from his parents and continues to search for them. The story is based on true events of the Second World War.

2. *Tom Sawyer* by Mark Twain
   You must try the famous story of Tom Sawyer who played by the Mississippi with Jim and Huckleberry Finn. It is one of the all time great stories!

3. *Otter Three Two Calling* by Leif Hamre
   Exciting adventure as five men of the Royal Norwegian Air Force are forced to land in the north of Norway. They face a struggle for survival in winter. This story was voted the best children's book of its year in Norway.

To write about

At the beginning of the story 'Journey's End' the writer tells how they came to the island.
'A rickshaw and a rowing-boat and a cargo boat and two country boats and a bus and a buffalo cart and this canoe. And the tide.'

Imagine you have made a similar journey.
Can you write a story of how you came to travel in so many different ways?
If you wish you could write your story in the form of a diary.

Canoe Story

We went in a long canoe, two of us.
He sat at the front, one of us.
I sat at the back, one of us.
We went in a long canoe, two of us.

Water whispered, 'I'm cool, ever so.'
Sun sang, 'I'm hot, hot.'
Breeze sighed, 'I'm not.'
Paddle said, 'Heave ho, ever so.'

He sat, his back to me, and paddled.
I sat, looked at his back, and dandled
My paddle on my knees, and dabbled
My hands, while he talked and babbled
And pushed and paddled and paddled, and paddled.

And paddled. And sweated. And puffed.
I was cool as the water.
He was hot as the sun.
He puffed, heave ho. I sighed, just so.

Sweating and puffing, he turned
And saw my paddle, at rest, on the floor, all alone,
My paddle, dry as a bone.
And he burst. He might have cursed.

He might have cursed, but I grabbed my paddle,
And I paddled and pushed, and poked and thrust,
And we skimmed, bubble-brimmed, across the lake,
While he sat and relaxed and cooled in the breeze.

And I gasped, 'It's hot.'
He smiled, 'I'm not.'
And I said, 'You look cool, ever so.'
And he turned and smiled, 'Heave ho, just so.'

                            Geoffrey Summerfield

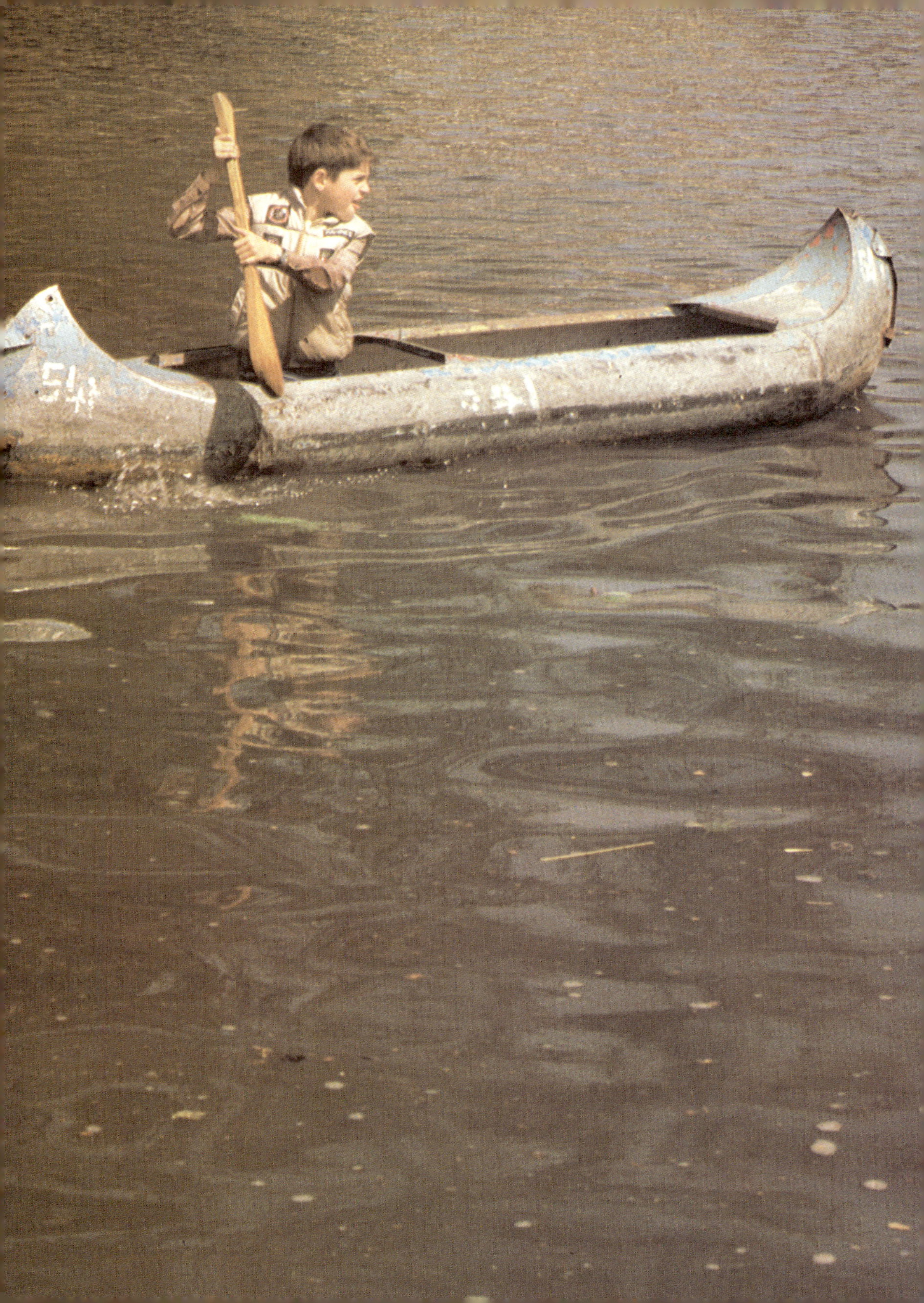
54

Searching for missing words

In the passage some words have been missed out.
Can you be sure which words have been missed out?
Sometimes there can be only one answer.
Sometimes there can be several answers for you to think and talk about.
How many words can you find?

    The driver, a fair-haired girl, was still unaware of his sudden arrival in her car. Flavio lay back and relaxed on the cushions. He stretched his back, and each leg in turn, to make sure he wasn't hurt. He was _____ unharmed. So he started to wash himself, _____ he thought what to do next.
    'Bit _____, wasn't it? You OK?' enquired a croaky _____ from the corner of the back seat.
    _____, who hadn't really had time to collect _____, nearly jumped out of his skin.
    'S'all _____. I'm only a tortoise. I belong to _____ nibs there.' The beady black eyes indicated the _____ of the Fiat: the girl was still _____ on driving through the congested traffic. Flavio made _____ the beautifully polished shell, the scaly _____ neck and the bright eyes that were _____ at him inquisitively.
    'I'm purr-fectly all right,' _____ Flavio, in the ruffled tones of one _____ has been caught unawares.

From *Flavio and the Cats of Rome* by Pamela Binns

Points of view

Here are some facts about an incident which took place in a supermarket.

The Crash

Fiona and Derek are bored waiting for their parents to gather the week's groceries. Derek starts to throw a ball to Fiona. Fiona throws the ball back rather too hard. Derek misses the catch and the ball completely knocks over a display stand full of dishes and glass-ware. The manager appears and grabs the two children. People stare and their parents arrive on the scene.

Imagine you are

    (a) either Fiona or Derek
or (b) the shop manager
or (c) one of the parents.

Could you give or write an account of the incident from your point of view?

Going to the library

Jennifer went off one day to the public library. She had been reading a very exciting book by a writer called Andrea Booth and she wanted to obtain another of this writer's books.
Would the library have it?
Jennifer looked at the fiction section. All the books were placed on the shelf in alphabetical order according to the author's surname.

BACON, William — *The Long Day*
BADDELEY, Eve — *Too Many Cooks*
BELL, Georgina — *William and the Turtle*
BENN, Fraser — *Space Flight Seventy Three*
BILBOW, Susan — *Jane and Her Friends*
BURROWS, Annette — *Oranges For Tea*
CURRAN, Hugh — *No Time Like Now*

But no book at all by Andrea Booth. What a pity!

Then Jennifer had a brainwave. She asked an assistant for help. 'Well, let's look here,' said the assistant. She took Jennifer over to a set of boxes with cards, each with the name of an author and the book the author had written.
The boxes were marked like this:

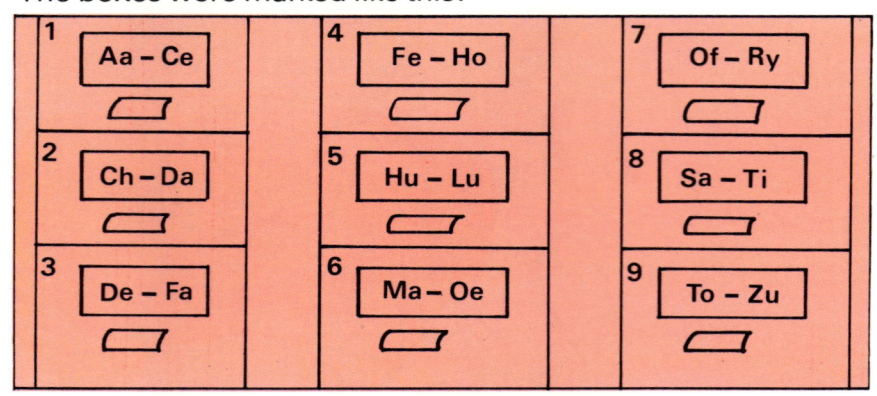

1 Aa – Ce	4 Fe – Ho	7 Of – Ry
2 Ch – Da	5 Hu – Lu	8 Sa – Ti
3 De – Fa	6 Ma – Oe	9 To – Zu

Sure enough, in Box 1 there was a card for a book by Andrea Booth called *Still Waters*.

'Well, Jennifer,' said the assistant, 'we have that book, but someone must have borrowed it. Call back next week and we'll see if it is in.'

Isn't that a useful set of boxes?

Which box would you look in for books by these writers?

Howard Thomson   **Alvin Norwood**
Emily Hardy   **Pearl Preece**
Derek Wilson   **George Barry**
Sarah Emerson   **Alice Jarrold**

Funny words

What word do you think the artist has drawn in this picture?

There are lots of words which are funny if you think about them. Talk about how you might make a funny drawing of the word

handrail

Can you draw a picture for **handrail**?

Fact or opinion?

Here is part of a conversation which is made up of a mixture of facts and opinions.

Jason is trying to persuade Helen to lend him her new bicycle.
　'Look Helen, you're a kind, generous, thoughtful sister …'
　'What do you want?' interrupted Helen.
　'Well,' continued Jason. 'Monday is a holiday and a few of my friends are planning to cycle over to the new swimming baths.'
　'I suppose by your "friends" you mean Charlie and Bill. Those two don't know how to look after anything.'
　'But they won't be near your bicycle and you know mine has a twisted front wheel,' pleaded Jason.
　'Yes and how did your front wheel get twisted?' asked Helen.
　'Oh Bill was unlucky — it was an accident. Could have happened to anyone! How was he to know about that pothole?'
　'It's funny how accidents always occur when Bill and Charlie are around. They must be the most accident-prone people in town.'
　'They're really great lads, Helen, and I promise not to give them a go. Come on. I won't be able to go unless you help. I'll always be grateful.'

Make a list of the **facts** you can find.
Make a list of the **opinions** you can find.
Do you think Helen will give in?

Read and remember

Can you read carefully and remember what you've read? Here is a short story. Read carefully and try to remember the order of events as they are told in the story. Do you think you'll remember when you turn to page 77?

The Treasure Seekers

Every morning for weeks the treasure seekers came out of the hotel as soon as dawn broke. They had detectors, spades, picks and food for the day's work. All this happened because a farmer found some valuable Roman coins in the area. They were a silent group, jealous of each other and determined to make the big strike. From time to time a cry would go up and this indicated that someone had found something of interest. Usually this discovery turned out to be an old tin can or bottle.

Now turn to page 77.

Spot the howler

The frogman swam along with his aqualung shining a torch.

Can you say what is wrong with this sentence?

I killed the fly with the spray which was annoying us.

Help! Help!

Everyone should have a full rice-bowl
And a thatch over their head.

You can't say very much more.
Life is a war that begins at the font
(Who can use any more war?).
In a world of wishes and want
There is a limit to what one can do.

Freedom grows and dwindles,
It dwindles and grows.
Happiness cannot be ordered,
It comes or it goes.

But at least, if least we must say,
Everyone should have a full rice-bowl
And a thatch over their head.
A job for the day,
For the night a bed.

                              D. J. Enright

To talk and write about

1. The story 'Journey's End' finishes with the writer meeting his uncle.
   Read again the last four or five paragraphs.
   What do you imagine happens next?
   Is Uncle Ahmed glad to meet his nephew?
   What now happens to Khoka?
   How do the two boys manage to stay on the island?
   Imagine you are either Apu or Khoka and write your story according to what you think happens to each.

2. The writer of 'Journey's End' had to leave his island for some reason.
   Imagine everyone in the town or area you live in has to leave because of some great danger.
   Call your story 'Danger in Delay'.

3. The writer of 'Journey's End' describes a crowd of people gathered round a dark green tent.
   Read this description again.
   Now write a description of a similar crowded place — perhaps a market place or the crowd at a sporting event.
   Try to describe very carefully the people in your crowded place.

Reading for the main idea

Mark was working on a project about **coal** and came across this passage in a book.

Millions of years ago the land of Britain was covered with great forests which grew out of the swampy ground. When this vegetation died and sank beneath the mud and sand, other trees grew in their place until they too died and sank. Eventually many layers of dead vegetation were pressed down into the ground, one on top of the other, to be covered by earth, mud, and gravel. It was a long slow process that continued for thousands of years until these decayed trees and plants hardened into the substance we know and use today — coal. Proof of this amazing process is shown by the many fossils found in the coal which has been mined. Imprints of tree bark, leaves, and ferns have been discovered in the coal dug up by the miners.

Mark made notes of the main ideas in the story. Here is what he wrote:

millions of years ago — huge forests — layers of dead trees.

Think of the other main ideas in the story.
Add them to Mark's list so that you have notes of all the main ideas.
Can you use your notes to write your own shortened version of the passage — 'Coal'?

Act it out

The Desert Island Game

This game is about being shipwrecked on a desert island. In it there are three survivors who have been washed ashore. They must be as different from each other as possible. Here are three to start with.

Jim Brown is the navigating officer of the ship which has just gone down. The others know he is an officer from the ship, but no more. Jim is always getting things wrong.

Priscilla Spratt is the ten-year-old daughter of a millionaire who was on a cruise on the ship. She is a very spoiled child, used to having everyone do as she wants, and to getting what she wants, when she wants it.

Mrs Agnes-Lucie Phogg is a very old lady who is slightly deaf. She believes that children should be 'seen and not heard'. She is also used to getting her own way and will blackmail others by saying how old and weak she is. In fact she is not weak at all.

What will happen? Can you make a short sketch about the three characters being washed ashore together?
Can you think of three more characters to be washed ashore? Try to make another quite different sketch about the characters you have made up.

To write about

Talk about this picture.
Imagine you are the child.
Could you tell a story about what you think is going to happen to you?

Read and remember

Can you put the sentences below in the same order as they came in the story 'Treasure Seekers' on page 71?
Don't look back to the original story.

(a) The treasure seekers were a silent jealous group.

(b) Now and then a cry would show someone had found something.

(c) As dawn broke the treasure seekers came outside.

(d) The treasure seekers had come because a farmer had found valuable coins.

(e) They had metal detectors, spades, picks and food with them.

(f) The treasure seekers usually only found rubbish like tin cans.

The company words keep

Jacqueline's class was given the word **eat** and asked to think of as many words as they could which would describe how someone or something might eat.
Here are their answers:

hungrily	**horribly**	**politely**
daintily	**fast**	**quietly**
messily	**quickly**	**noisily**

Can you think of more?
Do the same for the words

run   **smile**

Here is a poem written by a child who didn't enjoy a journey.

The Journey

Slowly, at first, the train moves off
Nobody talks,
Eyes wander round the carriage
But they don't often meet
And when they do they fly quickly
Outside or back to the newspaper
So the train moves on — faster now
Nobody saying much
Until at last we reach Aunt Millie's town
Thank goodness the boring journey is over!

Can you write a poem about a journey you remember?

Giving instructions

As part of her cycling proficiency test, Rita wrote these instructions for turning right on a bike.

1. Look over your shoulder to see that there is nothing coming from behind.
2. If nothing is coming, then move over so that you are cycling just to the left of the centre of the road.
3. Look ahead to see if anything is coming.
4. If something is coming, then stop and wait until it has passed. When nothing is coming, then it is safe to turn.

Talk about what Rita has written. Has she missed anything out? Can you improve on Rita's instructions?

Now think of another manoeuvre on a bike, or on foot in traffic. (Some suggestions are given below.)
Make-up a set of instructions for performing the manoeuvre you decide on.
Suggestions:
    turning left or right on a bike at traffic lights
    turning left or right at a 'Give Way' or 'Stop' sign
    how to negotiate a roundabout on a bike
    how to use a pedestrian crossing
    how to cross a road.

The way words are built

There are many interesting surnames.
Some have fascinating explanations behind them.
Talk about the surnames given below, and what you think the explanations behind them may be.

Underwood   **Jolly**

Cruikshanks   **Shakespeare**

White	Fox	Archer
Grey	Nutt	Hall
Swan	Moore	Miller

Could there be an interesting explanation behind your surname?
Do you know of any other interesting surnames?

UNIT 22

This story is taken from the book *Walkabout* by James Vance Marshall.

Two children

It was silent and dark, and the children were afraid. They huddled together, their backs to an outcrop of rock. Far below them, in the bed of the gully, a little stream flowed inland — soon to peter out in the vastness of the Australian desert. Above them the walls of the gully climbed smoothly to a moonless sky.

The little boy nestled more closely against his sister. He was trembling.

She felt for his hand, and held it, very tightly.

'All right, Peter,' she whispered. 'I'm here.'

She felt the tension ebb slowly out of him, the trembling die gradually away. When a boy is only eight a big sister of thirteen can be wonderfully comforting.

'Mary,' he whispered, 'I'm hungry. Let's have something to eat.'

The girl sighed. She felt in the pocket of her frock, and pulled out a paper-covered stick of barley sugar. It was their last one. She broke it, gave him half, and slipped the other half back in her pocket.

'Don't bite,' she whispered. 'Suck.'

Why they were whispering they didn't know. Perhaps because everything was so very silent; like a church. Or was it because they were afraid; afraid of being heard?

For a while the only sounds were the distant rippling water over stone, and the sucking of lips round a diminishing stick of barley sugar. Then the boy started to fidget, moving restlessly from one foot to another. Again the girl reached for his hand.

'Aren't you comfy, Pete?'

'No.'

'What is it?'

'My leg's bleeding again. I can feel the wet.'

She bent down. The handkerchief that she had tied round his thigh was now draped like a recalcitrant garter over his ankle. She refastened it, and they huddled together, holding hands, looking into the powdery blackness of the Australian night.

They could see nothing. They could hear nothing — apart from the lilt of the rivulet — for it was still too early for the stirring of bush life. Later there'd be other sounds; the hoot of the mopoke, the mating howl of the dingo, and the leathery flip-flap-flip of the wings of flying foxes. But now, an hour after sunset, the bush was silent: frighteningly still: full, to the children, of terrors all the greater for being unknown. It was a far cry from here to their comfortable home in Charleston, South Carolina.

The hours meandered past like slow, unhurrying snails. At last the boy's head dropped to his sister's lap. He snuggled closer. His breathing became slower, deeper. He slept.

But the girl didn't sleep; that would never have done; for she had to keep guard. She was the elder. The responsibility was hers. That was the way it had always been, as far back as she could remember. Always she had been the big sister who had stuck plaster on Peter's knees, had taught him to tie his shoe laces, and had taken the lead in their games of Indians and cowboys. Now that they were lost — somewhere in the middle of an unknown continent — the weight of her responsibility was greater than ever. A wave of tenderness welled up inside her. Always she had big-sistered him; now she must mother him as well.

For a while she sat staring into the darkness; the darkness that was warm, thick and almost tangible; soon her mind became utterly blank. The day's events had been too overwhelming; had drawn on her too heavily. The rhythmic beat of the small boy's slumber came to her lullingly now. Gradually her breathing fell in step with his. The whisper of the creek came to her like the croon of a lullaby. Her eyelids drooped and closed, fluttered and closed again. Soon she too was fast asleep.

In the darkness beyond the gully, the bush came slowly to life.
A lumbering wombat came creeping out of his ground den. His short stumpy body forced a way through the underscrub; his long food-foraging snout ploughing through the sandy earth in search of his favourite roots. Suddenly he stopped: sniffed: his nostrils dilated. He followed the strange new scent. Soon he came to the gully. He looked the children over; thoughtfully, not hungrily, for he was a vegetarian,

an eater of roots. His curiosity satisfied, he shambled slowly away.

Random fireflies zigzagged by; their nightlights flickering like sparklets from a roving toy-sized forge.

Soon creeping along the edge of darkness, came another creature: a marsupial tiger-cat, her eyes widened by the night to glowing oriflames of fire. She too had scented the children; she too clambered into the gully and looked them over. They smelt young and tender and tempting; but they were large; too bulky, she decided, to drag back to her mewling litter. On velvet paws she slunk away.

A night mist tried to gather: failed — for the air in the gully was too warm — and dissipated into pre-dawn dew. The dampness settled on the children, pressing down their clothes, tracing the outline of their bodies in tiny globules of pearl. They stirred but didn't wake. They were lost in their dreams.

In her sleep the girl moved uneasily. She was in the aeroplane again, and she knew that something was wrong. She and Peter were the only passengers, sandwiched between the crates of vegetables and the frozen carcasses of beef, and she was watching the port engine, waiting for the flames she knew would come. Too soon they were there; the tiny tongues of red licking out of the cowling. In her sleep she twisted and moaned; then mercifully, her mind went blank — nature's safety valve that protects, even in dreams, those who have been shocked beyond endurance — and the next thing she dreamt was that she and Peter were staggering away from the blazing plane, she pulling him frantically because one of his legs was numb and his feet kept sinking into the soft, yielding sand. 'Quick, Peter,' she gasped. 'Quick, before it explodes.' She heard a dull pulsating roar, and looking back saw the figure of the Navigating Officer carrying the pilot and clambering out of the wreckage. In the heat of the explosion he glowed white-hot, disintegrating. Again her mind went numb, but in her sleep she clutched her brother's hand; clutched it and squeezed it so tight that he half-woke and slid awkwardly off her lap.

To think and talk about

A 1. In what ways does Mary 'mother' Pete?
   2. Why was Peter trembling at the beginning of the story?
   3. Are there many people nearby? How do you know?
   4. Are there any other survivors? How do you know?

B 1. How well do you think the children will cope with the situation they are in?
   2. Where do you think the children were going when the plane crashed?
   3. The story emphasises the comfort Pete gets from having his sister there. Might the opposite also happen?
   4. Pete has been physically injured. Do you think Mary is injured in any way at all? In what way could she be hurt?

C 1. Imagine you are Mary. What will you do when daylight comes?
   2. Imagine you are Pete. How can you help Mary?
   3. The author sets the dark, silent scene at the start of the story, and gives us an idea of the fear of the children.
   How well does he do this?
   Can you find examples which show good ways of putting these ideas across?
   4. The story 'Two Children' is the very beginning of the book, *Walkabout*. Having read it, would you like to read more of the book? Why?

More books to read

1. *Hunter's Gold* by Roger Simpson
   Scott Hunter's father fails to return from the gold fields and Scott runs off in search of him. A series of exciting adventures set in New Zealand then follows.

2. *Doctor Hunger and Captain Thirst* by Meredith Hooper
   In trying to explore Australia two threats were never far away — hunger and thirst. These amazing stories of the men who explored Australia are well worth reading.

3. *Hills End* by Ivan Southall
   What should have been a happy picnic for everyone in Hills End turned into a nightmare for the seven who were exploring caves nearby. Read how a tremendous storm left the children to survive by their own efforts.

Shortened words

Sonja noticed that there are two ways to show when words have been shortened.

1. **We're going out today.**

In this sentence **we're** means **we are**, but you would *not* read it as **we are**.

2. **Mr. Brown is going out.**

In this sentence **Mr.** means **Mister**, and you *would* read it as **Mister**.

Write each of the following out in full.

Feb.	isn't	m.p.g.
Mon.	m.	Dr.
can't	U.K.	won't
kg.	wouldn't	s.a.e.

How would you read each of them?

To talk and write about

Imagine that you have recently moved to a new area. You are at a new school and although you have made some friends, there is someone in your class who takes pleasure in making your life a misery. You do all you can to make this person stop, but nothing seems to work.
What will you do?
Write the story.

Searching for missing words

In the passage some words have been missed out.
Can you be sure which words have been missed out?
Sometimes there can be only one answer.
Sometimes there can be several answers for you to think and talk about.
How many words can you find?

They took both his hands and led him through the little round-topped tunnels, following the lights which showed them the way to go to Charing Cross. A blast of warm air touched their already hot _____ as they walked down the steps onto the _____ and Kate had to hold on to _____ school beret to stop it blowing away. _____ fat woman who had been standing nearby _____ away hurriedly when she saw them, and Kate _____ not to notice. There was a distant _____ and Mr Trevellick started to shiver and _____, but the children held on to him _____ and although he went alarmingly stiff, he _____ his ground as the winking red eyes _____ the train appeared in the mouth of the _____ and then its long red body wound _____ way alongside the platform. The door slipped _____ and Mr Trevellick was bundled inside.

From *Travelling Magic* by R. H. Davis

Points of view

Here are some facts about an incident which takes place on a Saturday afternoon.

The Queue

A film that you have been waiting to see for a long time finally arrives at your local cinema. You and two friends decide to go on Saturday afternoon. When you arrive there is a long queue. It moves forward slowly. Five minutes before the film starts you are almost at the door when two people push into the queue in front of you. Just then the cinema manager comes out and announces, 'Ten more only'. Your friends and the two who pushed in get tickets, but you are left outside.

Imagine that you are

    (a) left outside
or (b) one of the people who pushed in
or (c) one of your friends.

Could you give an account of the incident from your point of view?

Kangaroo

... Delicate mother Kangaroo
Sitting up there rabbit-wise, but huge, plumb-weighted,
And lifting her beautiful slender face, oh! so much more gently
    and finely lined than a rabbit's, or than a hare's,
Lifting her face to nibble at a round white peppermint drop
    which she loves, sensitive mother Kangaroo.

Her sensitive, long, pure-bred face.
Her full antipodal eyes, so dark,
So big and quiet and remote, having watched so many
    empty dawns in silent Australia.

Her little loose hands, and drooping Victorian shoulders.
And then her great weight below the waist, her vast pale belly
With a thin young yellow little paw hanging out, and straggle
    of a long thin ear, like ribbon,
Like a funny trimming to the middle of her belly, thin little
    dangle of an immature paw, and one thin ear.

Her belly, her big haunches
And, in addition, the great muscular python-stretch of her tail.

There, she shan't have any more peppermint drops.
So she wistfully, sensitively sniffs the air, and then turns, goes
off in slow sad leaps

On the long flat skis of her legs,
Steered and propelled by that steel-strong snake of a tail.

Stops again, half turns, inquisitive to look back.
While something stirs quickly in her belly, and a lean little
    face comes out, as from a window,
Peaked and a bit dismayed,
Only to disappear again quickly away from the sight of the
    world, to snuggle down in the warmth,
Leaving the trail of a different paw hanging out ...

                                      D. H. Lawrence

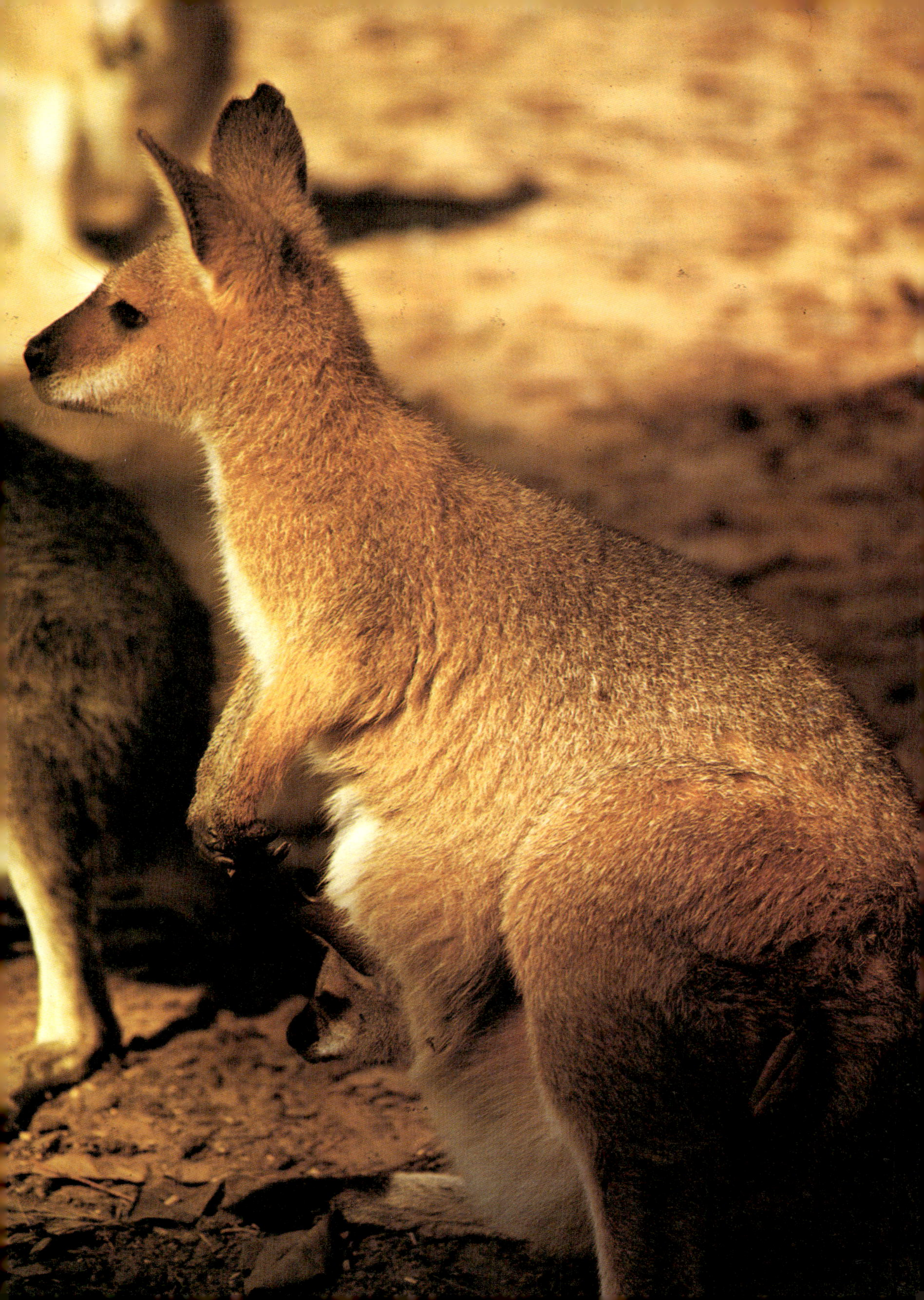

Sort it out

Here are groups of sentences which make a story.
They are in the wrong order.
Can you write the stories in the correct order?

1. (a) Karen soon noticed that it was full of creatures cut off by the tide.

   (b) The morning's fishing began and before long the jar was filled.

   (c) Starfish, crabs and lots of other creatures she couldn't put a name to, swam about or hid under rocks.

   (d) Paul produced his net and jar.

   (e) Karen, Paul and Patricia wandered down the beach one morning towards a rock pool.

   (f) Later the youngsters decided to see what other treasure had been washed ashore by the endless ebb and flow of the tide.

2. (a) The stranger wandered up to the bar coolly glancing round at the silent faces.

   (b) All this time the silence continued and suspicious eyes followed the stranger.

   (c) Usually the conversation continued when the newcomer was recognised.

   (d) On this occasion, however, the silence continued.

   (e) Quietly he asked for a room, signed his name in a battered book and climbed the stairs.

   (f) Only when he had disappeared upstairs did the murmur of conversation slowly begin again.

   (g) People stopped talking as the door opened.

Fact or opinion?

Have you ever been to a street market? If you have you're bound to have spent some time listening to the sellers trying to persuade people to buy.
Here is a sample of what you might hear in a London street market.

'OK folks, gather round and be amazed! Yes amazed! You'll probably think I should be locked up when you see the bargain I have here for you today. Now what do you think of that — one large bottle of the best perfume. Note the label madam. None of your rubbish this. If you can buy this stuff for less than £10 in your local high street then ... I'm a Dutchman. And what do I want for it? Not ten pounds, not nine, not even eight — half price £5. And because you're such a nice bunch of people I'll throw in this bottle of after-shave for your old man! Step right up — this is a once in a lifetime offer!'

Can you note all the **facts** in this passage?
Can you note all the **opinions** in this passage?

Weary Will

The strongest creature for his size
But least equipped for combat
That dwells beneath Australian skies
Is Weary Will the Wombat.

He digs his homestead underground,
He's neither shrewd nor clever;
For kangaroos can leap and bound
But wombats dig for ever.

The boundary-rider's netting fence
Excites his irritation;
It is to his untutored sense
His pet abomination.

And when to pass it he desires,
Upon his task he'll centre
And dig a hole beneath the wires,
Through which the dingoes enter.

And when to block the hole they strain
With logs and stones and rubble,
Bill Wombat digs it out again
Without the slightest trouble.

The boundary-rider bows to fate,
Admits he's made a blunder,
And rigs a little swinging gate
To let Bill Wombat under.

So most contentedly he goes
Between his haunt and burrow:
He does the only thing he knows,
And does it very thorough.

                          A. B. Patterson

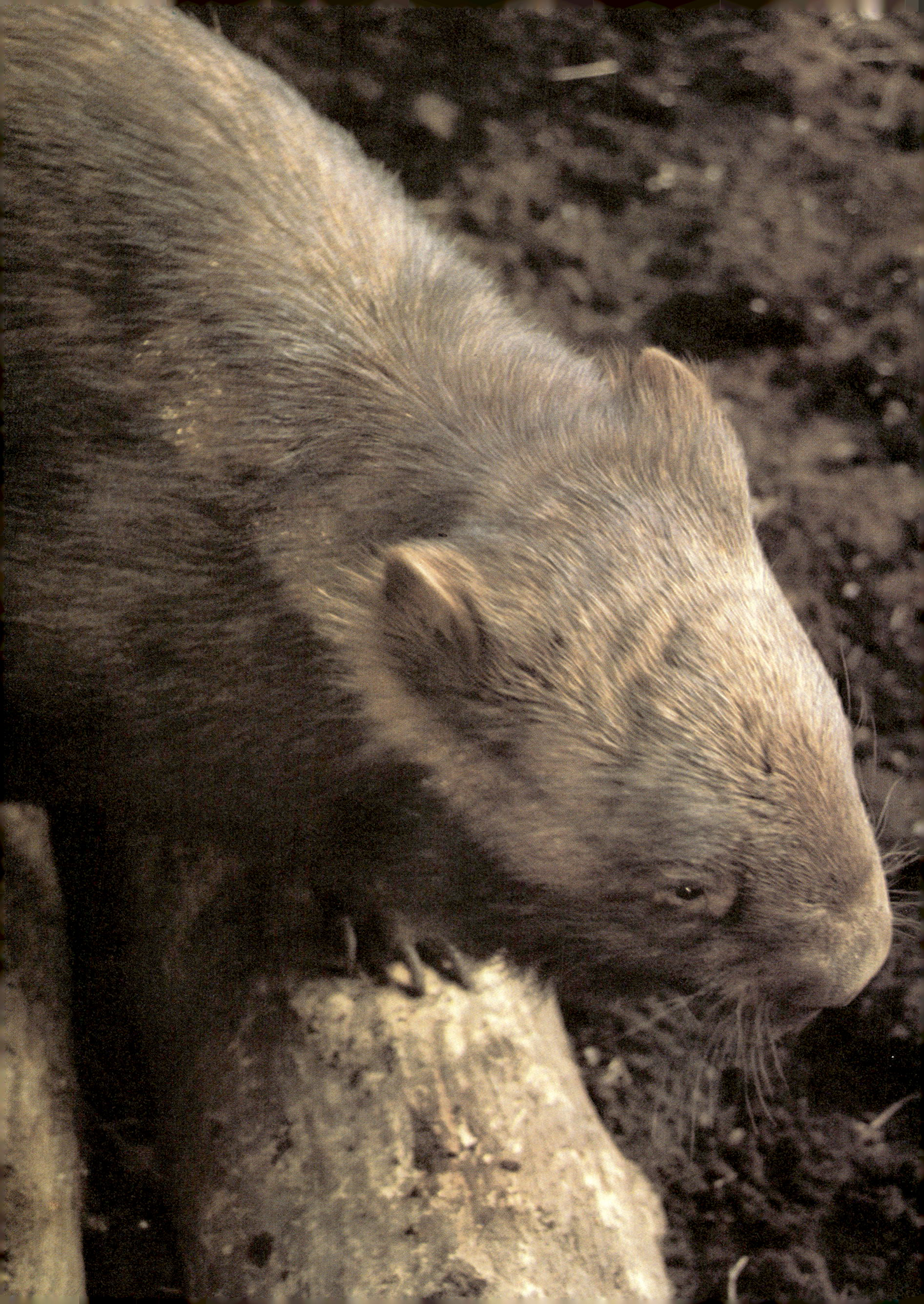

Read and remember

Can you read carefully and remember what you've read?
Read carefully and try to remember the order of events as they are told in the story.
Do you think you'll remember the order when you turn to page 103?

The Car Thief

Linda and Robert had been shopping and were on their way to the bus station. As they turned a corner Linda caught sight of a man trying to force open a car door. The two watched amazed as the man put a piece of wire in the window. Robert glanced across the road and ran to the phone box. Quickly he dialled 999 and gave all the information. A few minutes later a police car arrived and two policemen began questioning the man. Linda and Robert moved nearer and were embarrassed to hear the man explain how he had dropped his key down the nearby drain. The police apologised and helped the man get into his car.

Now turn to page 103.

Reading for the main idea

Carol was working on a project about **Helen Keller**. She came across this passage in a book.

As an infant, Helen Keller was left blind and deaf after an illness. Not being able to hear how others spoke, she could not imitate their sounds and was therefore herself unable to speak. She was an intelligent girl, but because of these problems she changed from a happy child into a bad-tempered girl with whom her parents found it difficult to cope. Desperately they sought help. Soon Helen had her own private teacher, Anne Sullivan. Having suffered from blindness in the past, Anne understood the problems facing Helen and was the ideal person to help her overcome them. It took years of effort and patience but both proved very determined in character and a deep bond grew between them. Anne taught Helen how to read Braille (an alphabet of raised dots used to teach the blind to read), how to write, and even how to speak.

Carol made notes of the main ideas in the story. Here is what she wrote:

Helen Keller — ill — blind and deaf
Helen — bad tempered.

Think of the other main ideas in the passage. Add them to Carol's list so that you have notes of all the main ideas.
Can you use your notes to write your own shortened passage about the story of Helen Keller?

To talk and write about

1. What are the night noises in your part of the world?
   Gill sat very quietly at the open window of her bedroom one night and noted the sounds she heard.
   She used the sounds to write a poem.

   > Train rushes down our valley.
   > Airliner overhead, straining, climbing.
   > Hush you car, baby's asleep.
   > But old Tom sings, savage, uncaring.

   What were the four sounds Gill used for her poem?
   Make your own night sounds into a poem.

2. Imagine that while on a journey you have become lost in a strange town.
   Where are you heading?
   Tell the story of how you get to your destination.

Using a dictionary

Use your dictionary to answer these questions by looking up the word in bold type in each sentence.

1. Why would you consult a **barrister** if you were in trouble with the law?
2. Why is a **cantaloupe** not likely to be found galloping in the plains of Africa?
3. If your father **disowned** you, would he be pleased with you? How do you know?
4. Would you be likely to **gambol** in a card game? Why?
5. If one of the tools of your trade were a **jemmy**, what would that trade be?
6. Would you be proud of being **notorious**? Why?
7. Would you trust someone who treated you in an **obsequious** way? Why?
8. Would you pay much attention to a **petty** complaint? Why?
9. If you are learning the **rudiments** of something, how much do you know about it already?
10. Do you think a **wizened** plum would look good to eat? Why?

Making Notes

Mary was in a hurry one day and she wrote the following list very quickly in her homework notebook. Each word with letters missed out has a full stop after it.

p. 68 maths. to no. 20.
fnsh. story abt. seasd.
rememb. netb. kit
trip to castle Aug. 16th.

Can you understand Mary's notes? Do you think she will be able to understand them herself?
It is very important to write enough to remind you about the things you want to remember.
Try writing a list like Mary's. It could be about many different things.

Spot the howler

The lamp shining on the child's face showed fear.

Can you say what is odd about this sentence?
We took the furniture out of the room as it was to be painted.

Read and remember

Can you put the sentences below in the same order as in the story 'The Car Thief' on page 98?
Don't look back to the story.

(a) The police arrived and asked the man questions.

(b) Linda and Robert had been shopping.

(c) Robert was quick to phone the police to tell them about the thief.

(d) It was Linda who first noticed a man breaking into a car.

(e) The police helped the man to get into his car.

(f) As they moved nearer they heard how the man had lost his key.

Act it out

A Nasty Problem

The Scene: You are walking down the street one day when you see a friend you have not seen for a few weeks. You call 'Hello', but instead of smiling and greeting you, your friend goes white and says, 'It can't be ... I was at your funeral only last week ... You're dead ...'
The Problem: How do you persuade your friend that you really are still alive?

Talk about how you could solve the problem.
Can you think of possible explanations for this happening?
What will happen?
Why not act 'A Nasty Problem' for your friends?

The way words are built

Posh

The word **posh** means 'smart' or 'spruced up'. There is an interesting explanation of how the word came about, which may be true.

In the days when India was part of the British Empire, many people went from Britain to India to work. The very rich got the best cabins on the ships, and always preferred to have a cabin which was away from the sun at midday, and would therefore be cooler. On the way out to India this would be on the port (left) side of the ship, and on the way back it would be on the starboard side. The word **posh** is said to be the initials of **P**ort **O**ut, **S**tarboard **H**ome.

UNIT 23

Charlie has been woken up by a fly. He thinks it has flown into his ear, and goes to wake his Mum, who looks and tells him that there is no fly in his ear and to go back to bed and stop imagining things.

'In the Middle of the Night' is from a book of short stories called *What the Neighbours Did*, by Phillipa Pearce.

In the middle of the night

'Good night,' said Mum from the darkness. She was already allowing herself to sink back into sleep again.

'Good night,' Charlie said sadly. Then an idea occurred to him. He repeated his good night loudly and added some coughing, to cover the fact that he was closing the bedroom door behind him — the door that Mum kept open so that she could listen for her children. They had outgrown all that kind of attention, except possibly for Wilson. Charlie had shut the door against Mum's hearing because he intended to slip downstairs for a drink of water — well, for a drink and perhaps a snack. That fly-business had woken him up and also weakened him: he needed something.

He crept downstairs, trusting to Floss's good sense not to make a row. He turned the foot of the staircase towards the kitchen, and there had not been the faintest whimper from her, far less a bark. He was passing the dog-basket when he had the most unnerving sensation of something being wrong there — something unusual, at least. He could not have said whether he had heard something or smelt something — he could certainly have seen nothing in the blackness: perhaps some extra sense warned him.

'Floss,' he whispered, and there was the usual little scrabble and snuffle. He held out his fingers low down for Floss to lick. As she did not do so at once, he moved them towards her, met some obstruction —

'Don't poke your fingers in my eyes!' a voice said, very low-toned and cross. Charlie's first, confused thought was that Floss had spoken: the voice was familiar — but then a voice from Floss should *not* be familiar; it should be strangely new to him —

He took an uncertain little step towards the voice, tripped over the obstruction, which was quite wrong in shape and size to be Floss, and sat down. Two things now happened. Floss, apparently having climbed over the obstruction, reached his lap and began to lick his face. At the same time a human hand fumbled over his face, among the slappings of Floss's tongue, and settled over his mouth. 'Don't make a row! Keep quiet!' said the same voice. Charlie's mind cleared: he knew although without understanding that he was sitting on the floor in the dark with Floss on his knee and Margaret beside him.

Her hand came off his mouth.

'What are you doing here, anyway, Charlie?'

'I like that! What about you? There was a fly in my ear.'

'Go on!'

'There was.'

'Why does that make you come downstairs?'

'I wanted a drink of water.'

'There's water in the bathroom.'

'Well, I'm a bit hungry.'

'If Mum catches you . . .'

'Look here,' Charlie said, 'you tell me what you're doing down here.'

Margaret sighed. 'Just sitting with Floss.'

'You can't come down and just sit with Floss in the middle of the night.'

'Yes, I can. I keep her company. Only at weekends, of course. No one seemed to realize what it was like for her when those puppies went. She just couldn't get to sleep for loneliness.'

'But the last puppy went weeks ago. You haven't been keeping Floss company every Saturday night since then.'

'Why not?'

Charlie gave up. 'I'm going to get my food and drink,' he said. He went into the kitchen, followed by Margaret, followed by Floss.

They all had a quick drink of water. Then Charlie and Margaret looked into the larder: the remains of a joint; a very large quantity of mashed potato; most of a loaf; eggs; butter; cheese . . .

'I suppose it'll have to be just bread and butter and a bit of cheese,' said Charlie. 'Else Mum might notice.'

'Something hot,' said Margaret. 'I'm cold from sitting in the hall comforting Floss. I need hot cocoa, I think.' She poured some milk into a saucepan and put in on the hot plate. Then she began to search for the tin of cocoa. Charlie, standing by the cooker, was already absorbed in the making of a rough cheese sandwich.

The milk in the pan began to steam. Given time, it rose in the saucepan, peered over the top, and boiled over on to the hot plate, where it sizzled loudly. Margaret rushed back and pulled the saucepan to one side. 'Well, really, Charlie! Now there's that awful smell! It'll still be here in the morning, too.'

'Set the fan going,' Charlie suggested.

The fan drew the smell from the cooker up and away through a pipe to the outside. It also made a loud roaring noise. Not loud enough to reach their parents, who slept on the other side of the house — that was all that Charlie and Margaret thought of.

Alison's bedroom, however, was immediately above the kitchen. Charlie was eating his bread and cheese, Margaret was drinking her cocoa, when the kitchen door opened and there stood Alison. Only Floss was pleased to see her.

'Well!' she said.

Charlie muttered something about a fly in his ear, but Margaret said nothing. Alison had caught them red-handed. She would call Mum downstairs, that was obvious. There would be an awful row.

Alison stood there. She liked commanding a situation.

Then, instead of taking a step backwards to call up the stairs to Mum, she took a step forward into the kitchen. 'What are you having, anyway?' she asked. She glanced with scorn at Charlie's poor piece of bread and cheese and at Margaret's cocoa. She moved over to the larder, flung open the door, and looked searchingly inside. In such a way must Napoleon have viewed a battlefield before victory.

Her gaze fell upon the bowl of mashed potato. 'I shall make potato-cakes,' said Alison.

They watched while she brought the mashed potato to the kitchen table. She switched on the oven, fetched her other ingredients, and began mixing.

'Mum'll notice it you take much of that potato,' said Margaret.

But Alison thought big. 'She may notice if some potato is missing,' she agreed. 'But if there's none at all, and if the bowl it was in is washed and dried and stacked away with the others, then she's going to think she must have made a mistake. There just can never have been any mashed potato.'

Alison rolled out her mixture and cut it into cakes; then she set the cakes on a baking-tin and put it in the oven.

Now she did the washing up. Throughout the time they were in the kitchen, Alison washed up and put away as she went along. She wanted

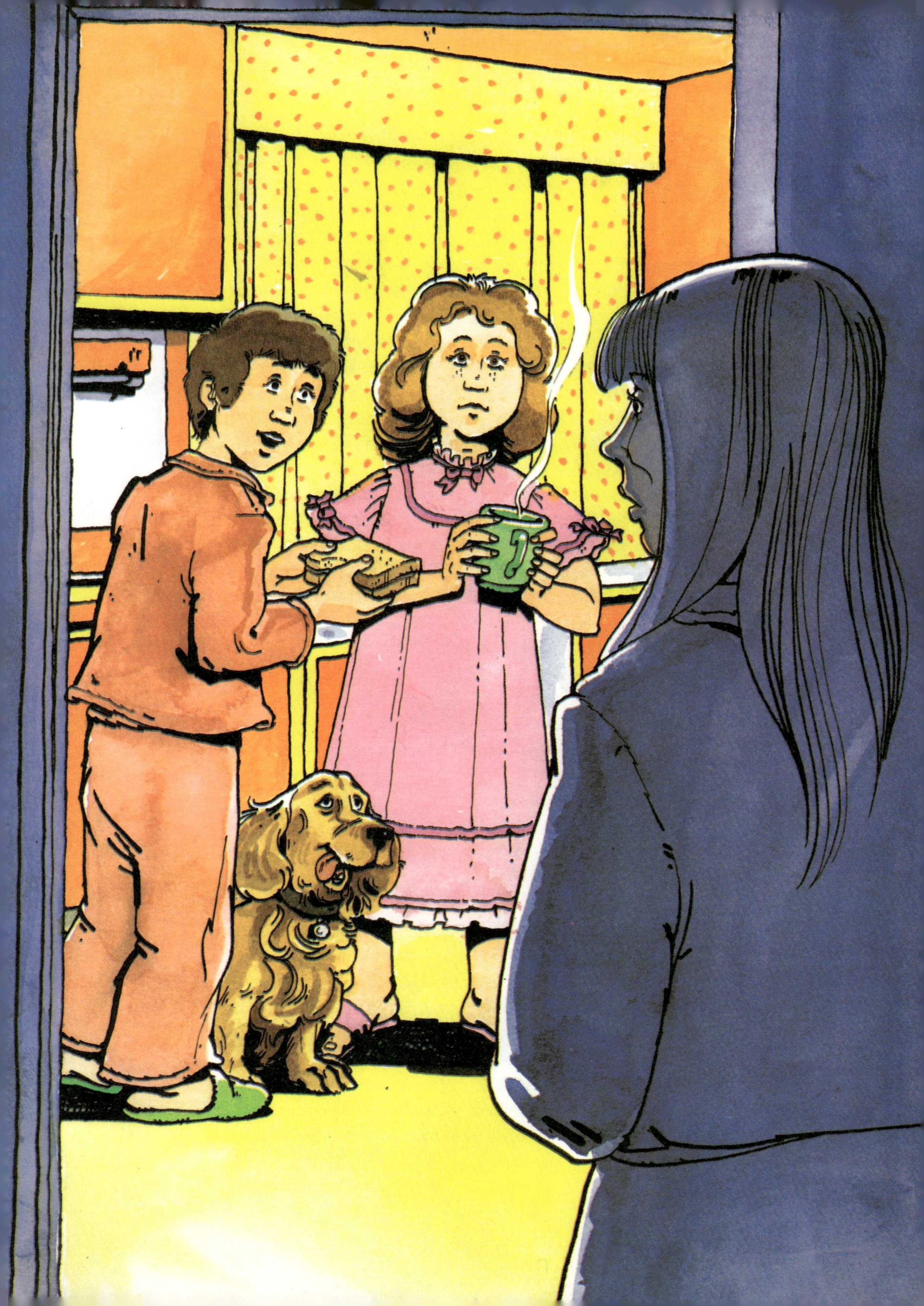

no one's help. She was very methodical, and she did everything herself to be sure that nothing was left undone. In the morning there must be no trace left of the cooking in the middle of the night.

'And now,' said Alison, 'I think we should fetch Wilson.'

The other two were aghast at the idea; but Alison was firm in her reasons. 'It's better if we're all in this together, Wilson as well. Then if the worst comes to the worst, it won't be just us three caught out, with Wilson hanging on to Mum's apron-strings, smiling innocence. We'll all be for it together; and Mum'll be softer with us if we've got Wilson.'

They saw that, at once. But Margaret still objected: 'Wilson will tell. He just always tells everything. He can't help it.'

Alison said, 'He always tells everything. Right: we'll give him something to tell, and then see if Mum believes him. We'll do an entertainment for him. Get an umbrella from the hall and Wilson's sou'wester and a blanket or a rug or something. Go on.'

They would not obey Alison's orders until they had heard her plan; then they did. They fetched the umbrella and the hat, and lastly they fetched Wilson, still sound asleep, slung between them in his eiderdown. They propped him in a chair at the kitchen table, where he still slept.

By now the potato-cakes were done. Alison took them out of the oven and set them on the table before Wilson. She buttered them, handing them in turn to Charlie and Margaret and helping herself. One was set aside to cool for Floss.

The smell of fresh-cooked, buttery potato-cake woke Wilson, as was to be expected. First his nose sipped the air, then his eyes opened, his gaze settled on the potato-cakes.

'Like one?' Alison asked.

Wilson opened his mouth wide and Alison put a potato-cake inside, whole.

'They're paradise-cakes,' Alison said.

'Potato-cakes?' said Wilson, recognizing the taste.

'No, paradise-cakes, Wilson,' and then, stepping aside, she gave him a clear view of Charlie's and Margaret's entertainment, with the umbrella and the sou'wester hat and his eiderdown. 'Look, Wilson, look.'

Wilson watched with wide-open eyes, and into his wide-open mouth Alison put, one by one, the potato-cakes that were his share.

But, as they had foreseen, Wilson did not stay awake for very long. When there were no more potato-cakes, he yawned, drowsed, and suddenly was deeply asleep. Charlie and Margaret put him back into his eiderdown and took him upstairs to bed again. They came down to return the umbrella and the sou'wester to their proper places, and to see Floss back into her basket. Alison, last out of the kitchen, made sure that everything was in its place.

The next morning Mum was down first. On Sunday she always cooked a proper breakfast for anyone there in time. Dad was always there in time; but this morning Mum was still looking for a bowl of mashed potato when he appeared.

'I can't think where it's gone,' she said. 'I can't think.'

'I'll have the bacon and eggs without the potato,' said Dad; and he did. While he ate, Mum went back to searching.

Wilson came down, and was sent upstairs again to put on a dressing-gown. On his return he said that Charlie was still asleep and there was no sound from the girls' rooms either. He said he thought they were tired out. He went on talking while he ate his breakfast. Dad was reading the paper and Mum had gone back to poking about in the larder for the bowl of mashed potato, but Wilson liked talking even if no one would listen. When Mum came out of the larder for a moment, still without her potato, Wilson was saying: '. . . and Charlie sat in an umbrella-boat on an eiderdown-sea, and Margaret pretended to be a sea-serpent, and Alison gave us paradise-cakes to eat. Floss had one too, but it was too hot for her. What are paradise-cakes? Dad, what's a paradise-cake?'

'Don't know,' said Dad, reading.

'Mum, what's a paradise-cake?'

'Oh, Wilson, don't bother so when I'm looking for something . . . When did you eat this cake, anyway?'

'I told you. Charlie sat in his umbrella-boat on an eiderdown-sea and Margaret was a sea-serpent and Alison —'

'Wilson,' said his mother, 'you've been dreaming.'

'No, really — really!' Wilson cried.

But his mother paid no further attention. 'I give up,' she said. 'That mashed potato: it must have been last week-end . . .'

To think and talk about

A 1. Does Alison usually join in the fun? How do you know?

2. Can you put the children in order of age, eldest first?

3. Are these children used to having everything done for them? How do you know?

4. 'Alison stood there. She liked commanding a situation.' What does this mean? How many examples can you find of Alison behaving in this way?

B 1. If Mum had come downstairs and found the four children, what do you think would have happened?

2. If Dad had come down, what do you think would have happened?

3. What sort of job do you think Alison will do when she grows up? Why?

4. Do the children treat their dog Floss well? Why do you think so?

C 1. Imagine you are Alison, finding the others in the kitchen. What thoughts go through your mind?
What would *you* have done?

2. Imagine you are Wilson.
How much of what went on do you understand?

3. Try to imagine 'In the Middle of the Night' as a true story. Are there any parts which you cannot believe would happen in real life?

4. Mum is obviously strict with the children. Do you think this is right, or should children be given more freedom than these children seem to have?

More books to read

1. *The Mouse and his Child* by Russell Hoban
   About the great struggle of the clockwork mouse and his offspring to become self-winding, and the wicked Manny Rat who seeks to destroy them.

2. *Bedknob and Broomstick* by Mary Norton
   Imagine finding a magic bedknob which allows you to travel into the past. That's what happens to Charles, Cary, and Paul.

3. *Five Children and It* by E. Nesbit
   The first of three books about the same family. If you enjoy reading how children discover secret magic then you'll have a lot of good reading to do.

Ideas to write about

1. Most people have nights when they simply can't seem to get to sleep.
   Talk about what you think about when you can't get to sleep, and the things you can do to help yourself sleep.
   Write the story of a sleepless night.

2. Imagine you are Margaret, Charlie, or Alison. Wilson won't stop talking about the potato cakes, and you are afraid of being found out. How will you silence him?

3. Just imagine that it *was* Floss who spoke to Charlie!
   Write the story from the time when he found Floss could speak, as Charlie might tell it.
   Remember to make what you know about Floss fit into the story!

Searching for missing words

In the passage some words have been missed out.
Can you be sure which words have been missed out?
Sometimes there can be only one answer.
Sometimes there can be several answers for you to think and talk about.
How many words can you find?

The beach was full of completely white sand. The bay was like a half-moon stretching from one headland to the other, and it formed a trap for all that the winds swept round the island towards the leeward side. Driftwood lay _____ up at the high-water mark under the _____ bushes, but lower down on the beach _____ sand was empty and as smooth as a _____ floor. It was nice to walk on. _____ you walked along the edge of the _____, your paws left little holes that filled up _____, like springs. Moomintroll started to look for _____ for his mother, but the only ones _____ could see were broken. Perhaps they'd been _____ by the sea.

He saw something shining _____ the sand that wasn't a shell. It _____ a tiny little silver horseshoe. Quite close _____ there were hoof-marks in the sand, _____ straight into the sea.

From *Moominpappa at Sea* by Tove Jansson

Points of view

Here are a few facts about an incident which takes place one day in spring.

The Birthday Surprise

It is your father's birthday. As a surprise you and your sister decide to cut the grass in front of the house for him. It is nearly finished when a fire engine roars down the street, lights flashing. You forget to look where you are going and mow down your neighbour's favourite tulips. He comes rushing out of his house shouting furiously, just as your father gets back from work.

Imagine you are

- (a) one of the children
- **or** (b) the father
- **or** (c) the neighbour.

Could you give or write an account of the incident from your point of view?

To write about

What is going on in this picture?
Who is driving away in the car?
Who do you think the person at the window is?

Could you write the story of which this picture might be a part?

Read and remember

Can you read carefully and remember what you've read?
Here is a short story.
Read carefully and try to remember the order of events as they are told in the story.
Do you think you'll remember the order when you turn to page 126?

A Visit to the Pet Shop

Sandra had quite a bit of pocket money saved and decided to buy something for herself. As she wandered down the High Street trying to make up her mind she passed the pet shop. There in the window was a large white rabbit. Quickly the decision was taken, the money paid, and Sandra made her way home with the rabbit in a cardboard box. Her mother and father were at first very angry with Sandra. Eventually, however, Sandra's father went outside and quietly started to build a hutch. When mother gave her a few lettuce leaves Sandra knew that she would be allowed to keep her new friend whom she called 'Snowball'.

Now turn to page 126.

How to use a book

Many of the books in your classroom and in your school library have an **index**. An index is at the end of a book. It helps you to find things quickly in a book.

1. Here is a small part of an index from a book:

Flamingo	69	Food	134
Flax	32	Football	23
Flea	97	Ford, Henry	68
Fleming, Sir Alexander	103	Forests	59
Flight	43	Fossils	121
Flood	65	France	84
Florence	167	Fox	38
Flute	77	Frankenstein	193
Florida	45	Fraser River	92
Fog	100	Frost	52

(a) Are all the words in the correct alphabetical order?

(b) What kind of a book do you think this is?

(c) If you were looking up the writer A. A. Milne in an index would you look up A or M?

(d) How would your own name be entered in an index?

(e) On which page do you think you might find out more about the following? There may be more than one answer.

musical instruments   **our climate**
monsters   **travel**

2. Pick any three entries from the index page above.
   Can you find out more about each of them from a reference book in your classroom or school library?

3. Susan wanted to find out about a signal box. It was not in the index of the book she looked up, but it wasn't a very long index and she thought it might come under some other heading. She looked up **trains** and sure enough there was something about signal boxes.
   What do you think you might look up if these words were not in an index?

   butter   **terrier**   **picture**   **motor car**

Funny words

What word do you think the artist has made a drawing of in this picture?

There are lots of funny words. Talk about how you might make a funny drawing of the word

goldrush

Can you draw a funny picture for **goldrush**?

119

The Dark

I feared the darkness as a boy;
And if at night I had to go
Upstairs alone I'd made a show
Of carrying on with those below
A dialogue of shouts and 'whats?'
So they'd be sure to save poor Roy
Were he attacked by vampire bats.

Or thugs or ghosts. But far less crude
Than criminal or even ghost
Behind a curtain or a post
Was what I used to dread the most —
The always-unseen bugaboo
Of black-surrounded solitude.
I dread it still at sixty-two.

                        Roy Fuller

Giving instructions

Mark wrote the following set of instructions for a card game.

1. Deal the whole pack until there are no cards left. Players do not look at their cards, but keep them in a pile facing downwards.

2. Each player takes it in turn to turn up one card into a pile in the middle of the table.

3. This continues until two cards of either the same suit, or the same number have been played in succession.

4. The first person to notice that two like cards have been played shouts 'Snap!'

5. The first person to shout 'Snap!' collects all the cards in the pile, and turns them over, to add to the bottom of his own pile. The object of the game is to collect as many cards as possible. The winner is the first person to get the whole pack.

6. The game continues in the same way, until one person has the whole pack. If someone loses all their cards, they may continue to watch the game, and may shout once after losing their cards, to try to get back into the game.

Are there enough instructions?
Talk about Mark's instructions, and try to decide if there is anything which he has missed out.
Can you improve on Mark's instructions for playing Snap?

Choose another simple game, either from the list below, or one of your own choice.
Try to make up instructions for playing it, as Mark did for Snap.

| marbles | tig or tag | hopscotch |
| conkers | rounders | dodgeball |

Is it in the passage?

Cindy wrote this letter about **pollution** for her school magazine.

Dear Editor,

I suppose some of you are like me and haven't thought much about pollution. It isn't something many of us get very excited about. Yet we should take an interest in what's happening to our towns, cities, rivers and coasts.

   I started to take an interest when I was at my aunt's. She lives near the sea and I find it fun to play amongst the rocks near the shore. During my last visit, I was shocked to see birds lying dead near the shore. They were covered in oil. This terrible sight brought home to me just what the word *pollution* can mean. You've got to see for yourself before you'll really understand. From that day on I've been trying to look for ways to stop mankind ruining the world and I hope you will too. It's the only world we've got!

      Yours faithfully,
      Cindy

Put the sentences below into three groups:
   (a) Facts which are in the passage
   (b) Opinions which are in the passage
   (c) Facts or opinions which are NOT in the passage.

1. Most people don't think about pollution.
2. The author's aunt is worried about pollution.
3. Birds covered in oil have been found on some shores.
4. It is possible to read about pollution.
5. Reading about pollution is not the same as seeing for yourself.
6. Everyone should take an interest in pollution in cities, rivers and coasts.

7. We should stop using oil and stop killing birds.
8. We've only got one world in which to live.
9. Pollution will be stopped if we keep a watch on the world.
10. The author enjoyed being at the seashore.

Act it out

Alexa and her group thought the story 'In the Middle of the Night' would make a good play. They talked about what they thought the difficult parts would be. Here is some of what they said.

Alexa: It will have to be a quiet play, after all their Mum and Dad are upstairs asleep.
Maeve: We'll have to do everything as if it is dark . . .
Ronald: Will we have someone to play Floss, the dog?
Karl: Some of the actions will be hard to do . . .

What do you think of the children's points?
Can you see any more difficulties about acting the story?
How would you go about solving the problems?
Could you *write* a play of 'In the Middle of the Night'?
Try acting the play for your friends. Remember how you said you would solve the difficulties.

Reading for the main idea

Jill was working on a project about **nature** and came across this passage in a book.

Everyone marvels at the many wonders of Nature — the beauty of valleys, mountains, lakes, and forests; the wonderful variety of plant life and many colourful flowers; the insect, bird, and animal life and their habits, to name but a few.
   There is another side, however, not so pleasant. Like we humans, Nature has many moods — one moment gentle and peaceful like a lamb and, the next, like some raging ferocious beast, out to destroy all in its path. People cannot control it. They can only study and try to understand these things. In this way we can learn to be more on our guard to deal with these destructive forces of Nature which threaten us. Take, for example, the power of hurricanes, typhoons, and other strong winds! By forecasting where and when a hurricane will strike, we can help cut down the amount of damage caused by the destructive side of Nature.

Jill made notes of the main ideas in the story.
Here is what she wrote:

   — **everyone marvels at the wonders of nature**
   — **nature has many moods**.

Think of the other main ideas in the passage. Add them to Jill's list so that you have notes of all the main ideas.
Can you use your notes to write your own shortened passage about nature?